Cyprus, I Have Embraced Your Heart

Maria Andreas

Grateful thanks to Huge Jam (Jacqueline Tobin) who not only translated and edited this book but deeply shared every emotion and testimony, so that it is the true mirror of the original French version
Chypre, j'ai embrassé ton coeur!

First published in English by
Huge Jam, 2022

Copyright © 2022 Maria Andreas
All rights reserved.
ISBN: 978-1-7391829-0-8

To Pierre,
who followed his intuition
in bringing me to Cyprus.
And to Popi, my Cypriot sister.

*In memory of Georgia,
assassinated at twelve years old
on 25th December 1963
during intercommunity clashes in Nicosia.*

PROLOGUE

The Cyprus of 2022 has changed a lot. Supermarket prices are in line with those of continental Europe. Both young and old are addicted to social networks. Churches are no longer left open, especially when unattended, since vandals even steal metal from the tombstones. The courtyards of its monasteries are often crowded. Many close their doors very early and no longer accommodate pseudo-pilgrims. My monastery, where fortunately The Mother of God remains for eternity, is no longer what it was in the nineties. The oldest monks are in paradise; others have been sent to an old monastery to restore it. In summer the doors of houses are no longer wide open. Old women no longer watch TV from the street at night. And they no longer cross the city on Easter evening, their big purses in their hands.

The Cyprus that I am talking about and of which, fortunately, there are still traces, is the island that I discovered more than 27 years ago. While there may be inaccuracies in my memory, for which I beg my friends to forgive me, nothing has been invented by it. Everything has been lived. Except of course the historical part for which, once again, I would ask your indulgence for any errors.

The reader looking for a tourist guide will be disappointed. It is, and here I think the title is clear, a love story, not a travel agency brochure. However, I can recommend the region of Ayia Napa-Protaras with its superb beaches for "trendy" holidays; Paphos, for being more picturesque and historic; the Troodos mountains and their wild hiking trails; the city of Limassol, well-centred geographically with a very modern infrastructure. Finally, Larnaca; more peaceful, and that is my preference. Nature lovers will be able to recognise the seasons, when the geese pass over the island announcing winter, or when the flamingos settle on the salt lake as soon as the first heat comes.

I have deliberately chosen not to give any names[1] or indications of locations.

First to preserve the privacy of those I describe. Then to protect my own privacy. But above all because we do not give out the heart's address. We can only invite another heart to follow by instinct, by deciphering the winks of each one's unique destiny. It doesn't matter what the journey is, even if the choice is a pilgrimage into the unknown. A pilgrimage to the other...

Beyond that, and we must not shy away from this, there is also a very long way to go, before a few moments of grace can be enjoyed. For my part, the mastery of the Greek language is still an essential quest, because "the word is a living being"[2], as the great Victor Hugo said.

---

[1] With the exception of Georgia's, to whose memory this book is dedicated.
[2] Contemplations

PART ONE

The third largest island in the Mediterranean after Sicily and Sardinia, a strategic place between East and West, conquered and reconquered, it is not surprising that its hymn to freedom resounds with a particular ardour.

> *I recognise you by the edge*
> *of your fearsome sword;*
> *I recognise you by that quick glance*
> *That measures the earth.*
>
> *Springing from the bones*
> *The holiest of the Hellenes,*
> *Like the original bravery,*
> *I salute you, O Liberty, I salute you!*[3]

This Cypriot anthem, which is also the Greek anthem, permeates the soul of a people who have been plundered, oppressed, sold and colonised so

---

[3] Translated from Pierre Deschamps' French translation.

often. Of course, they are not alone in this and, as is often the case with such contested nations, the succession of tyrannies has also enriched the island, thanks to the different cultures that have crossed paths there.

I didn't want to write a living testimony, without evoking some flashes of history or legend. With the hope of triggering an emotion, that will prompt the reader to undertake further research, or even correct me.

In antiquity, Mycenaeans, Phoenicians, Egyptians, Assyrians, Persians succeeded each other on the island. Alexander the Great's victory over Darius earned him Cyprus, which had been fighting alongside the Persians. This marks the beginning of the Hellenization of the Island of Copper.[4]

The Greek gods also have their share of the Cypriot legend. Ouranos, after his union with Gaia was emasculated in his sleep by his son, the Titan Cronus. With the sickle his mother had given him to get rid of her husband. Ouranos' sex, when thrown into the sea, turned into a

---

[4] In Greek, 'cyprus' means 'copper'.

white foam from which, near Paphos, the goddess Aphrodite with her immaculate skin emerged. At the end of the Akamas peninsula, in an idyllic botanic garden, is the natural lake where the goddess of love liked to bathe. Thus sealing Beauty's pact with the island.

When Cyprus came under Roman rule in 58 BC, prosperity flourished thanks to the Pax Romana.

It was in Salamis[5] that the Levite Jew Joseph, nicknamed Barnabas, was born. Having become a Christian, he introduced Saint Paul to the apostles in Jerusalem. He then returned with him to his native island to anchor the roots of Christianity there forever. The first converted head of state was to be the Roman proconsul Sergius Paulus. But these are not the only men to have set down the roots of Christianity in the island of Aphrodite. It seems that Saint Andrew came there; a boat carrying his mother having been shipwrecked, near the north-eastern tip of the island. At the end of the cape that bears the name of the apostle, there is a famous monastery

---

[5] A town in the northern part of Cyprus.

dedicated to him. And of course Saint Lazarus, the Friend of Christ. After Christ's crucifixion, his relatives began to be persecuted. Saint Lazarus fled to Cyprus, some 400 kilometres from the holy city as the crow flies. He was consecrated as the first bishop of Larnaca by the apostles. According to Tradition, he lived there for about 30 years, before dying for a second time. It is said that he never smiled, and those who have seen his icon on the iconostasis of his cathedral know it. Although for tourists demanding a more jovial face, ridiculous portraits have been sold for the last few years. Too bad, because this is how the soul of a people evaporates little by little. Saint Lazarus, before being brought back to life, had stayed in Hades for four days. Just before Christ liberated souls from Hades, during what is commonly called in English The Harrowing of Hell. And the suffering that Saint Lazarus saw there meant that he never smiled again in his second life. As for the salt lake behind Larnaca, a legend says that it was once rich vineyards. One day as he passed by, a thirsty Saint Lazarus had asked for a bunch of grapes but was refused them by the winemaker.

So Saint Lazarus responded that from then on his vineyard would be transformed into a salt lake.

It is on the edge of this same salt lake, west of Larnaca, that the Hala Sultan Tekke mosque or mosque of Umm Haram stands. The most sacred Muslim place in Cyprus and the site of a famous pilgrimage. It houses the tomb of Umm Haram, Muhammad's nurse. Considered in Cyprus to have been his aunt, she was also one of his first disciples. It was she who persuaded the Prophet to let her accompany his followers to conquer the island. Despite Muhammad having prophesied she would die during that invasion. Around the year 650, already very old at the time of travelling, she fell from her mule and broke her neck. She was buried in this peaceful and preserved place. Above her grave is a block of stone which, according to legend, arrived miraculously from Jerusalem, from the sky.

The Byzantines between the 4th and 12th centuries have so impregnated the island with their culture that no occupant will ever be able to erase it. Especially so after the reconquest by

Emperor Nicephorus Phocas[6], that ended three centuries of Arab maritime supremacy. A culture inseparable from the Orthodox Church, which suffered the formidable yoke of its Roman Catholic brothers during the Crusades. The island – sold by Richard the Lionheart to the Knights Templar, who will resell it to Guy de Lusignan[7], King-elect of Cyprus – will become a base for the Crusaders. A period of economic development, but also of repression of the Byzantine culture. I cannot help speaking of the martyrdom, by their Roman Catholic brothers, of the thirteen monks of Kantara, in 1231. Arriving in Cyprus from the Holy Mountain[8], the Orthodox monks settled in the monastery of Kantara. Their ascetic virtues attracted so many devotees that the Roman Catholic archbishop decided to put an end to the popularity. He sent emissaries to impose on them something unthinkable to an Orthodox believer: unleavened bread for Eucharistic communion. I will not expand upon this vast subject here, but

---

[6] Byzantine Emperor, 912-969
[7] Lived 1153-1194, a nobleman from Poitier.
[8] Mount Athos, Greece

the Orthodox commune in the Body (bread) and Blood (wine) of Christ, and have done so since the first Holy Communion. The thirteen monks' hegumen suggested lighting a furnace and then performing their own traditional communion. After communion, each side – Roman Catholic and Orthodox – would enter the fire. Then it would be clear what Divine Truth thought of the bread. It's true that as a negotiation, it could have been better! Needless to say, the Roman Catholics refused. After a night of prayer, the monks travelled to Nicosia to present their arguments according to the Tradition of the Church Fathers. In the absence of an answer, the archbishop had them flogged, then thrown in prison. For three years of being subjected to frequent torture, starving in an icy dungeon, the thirteen monks did not give in. They were finally handed over to the executioners. To the mere observer, this suffering may seem unnecessary. My reason understands it, even shares it. But for the Orthodox, it is thanks to these testimonies, martyrs as "witnesses", that the services have been able to retain such a spiritual density. I experienced it in Saint Lazarus Cathedral. In the middle of the liturgy I would often say to myself: "If the Friend of Christ[9] is among the faithful, he will not be out of place! Hold on, believe in it and hold on!" This is undoubtedly what helped Cyprus survive the human trafficking inflicted by pirates; to the Venetians between 1485 and 1571, then to three centuries of Ottoman domination. Roman Catholic property is pillaged in its turn, serfdom abolished and the catholic clergy driven out. Not that the Ottomans preferred the Orthodox faith, because the latter too had its martyrs under their reign. But the only thing that mattered was that the taxes were collected, and that the flowers of youth were sent to the harems. Women as concubines, men as eunuchs. Everyone takes advantage of their victory, nothing new under the sun! Yet the vault of orthodoxy grew stronger, as is often the case during tough times. However, let us hope that, between exchanging messages on their mobile phones, the Cypriots of 2022 will not forget those who engraved the most beautiful of freedoms onto their land. Inner

---

[9] Saint Lazarus

freedom, whatever the outer conditions.

In 1878 the island was ceded by the Ottomans to the English as a protectorate, in exchange for a tribute, which is to say that it remained subject to the Ottoman empire. With the hope of closer alignment to Europe, especially Greece, and of being freed from haraç[10], the Greek Cypriots approved of the British arrival at first. In 1914, the latter completely annexed the island, which became a crown colony. At the beginning of the 20th century, the population was made up of around 18% Turkish Cypriots, on the island since the Ottoman occupation, and 80% Greek Cypriots. The Turks wanted a partition of the island, while the Greeks wanted to be attached to Greece. In 1950 the Cypriot Orthodox Church and 96% of Greek Cypriots voted for Enosis, which means reunification with Greece. The British obviously did not see that in a good light and even recruited Turkish Cypriots into the army. By creating a constitution in the 1950s, they gave the Turkish population (which then represented 18%) 30% of the parliamentary

---

[10] A very heavy tax on property, imposed on non-muslims

seats. Escalations in intercommunal violence followed. In 1955 the Greek Cypriots took up arms against the British and founded the EOKA[11] led by Georgios Grivas[12], assisted by Grigoris Afxentiou[13]. The latter committed numerous attacks against the empire which ended up offering money for his capture. Afxentiou whose story is told in the museum of the Machairas monastery, stopped at nothing. It even seems that he received the blessing to disguise himself as a monk, in order to escape the colonisers. Tragic end for this young hero who preferred death to surrender. Hidden in a cave in the Troodos near Machairas, betrayed by a Cypriot who no doubt collected the promised £5,000, he fought with his companions for more than ten hours. On March 3rd, 1957 he became a national hero when the British set fire to his cave and he burned to death. Two years later, the Zürich Agreements put an end to the anti-colonial struggle, and in 1960 the independence of Cyprus was finally achieved. "I salute you, O

---

[11] National Organisation of Cypriot Struggle
[12] 1897-1974
[13] 1928-1957

freedom, I salute you!" The United Kingdom, Turkey and Greece are the guarantors of constitutional balance. English military bases remain on 3% of the territory. Cyprus, new member of the Commonwealth joins the UN. Archbishop Makarios III becomes the first president, with a Turkish vice-president Fazil Küçük. The constitution guarantees that Turks will make up 30% of the civil service, 40% of the police force and have the right of veto in parliament. You didn't need to be a prophet to suspect that the balance would be precarious! Besides, Makarios is not fooled: "The agreements have created a state but not a nation!"[14] So it is that the island of Aphrodite will continue to feature at the forefront of the international situation for some time, even becoming a Cold War issue. All the while President Makarios receives support from developing countries and the USSR, while maintaining a policy of non-alignment. The oft-contested personality of Makarios is so intertwined with the contemporary history of Cyprus that I have

---

[14] 1963

chosen to continue my overview of the island's history with some more about this emblematic figure. On a personal note, when I was a kid, my mother couldn't stand him. At that time hostile to clerics, she fumed when she saw photos of Makarios at the UN or elsewhere. While for my part I found him lordly with his long black veil, as black as his big eyes. Surrounded by negotiators who seemed to me to have very bland faces. So there you go, my fascination with this island started at a very young age!

Before speaking a little about Makarios, however, I would like to say how hostile I am to a man of the church having any political power, the same with having a politician in ecclesiastical life. This opinion is also shared by many of my Cypriot friends. Questioned again recently, they told me how much they had appreciated the Archbishop, but not necessarily the President of the Republic. Circumstances are sometimes unavoidable; especially since the Byzantine tradition was threatened so often by the Ottomans, archbishops became accustomed to defending temporal goods as well. What an incredible destiny for this shepherd's son to be at times betrayed, adulated, hated, adored. For all great men, loneliness is their lot, and Makarios was no exception. No doubt the very private man also took secrets with him to his tomb which he had chosen to face East, close to the monastery of Kykkos. A simple and humble tomb, as he himself remained his whole life. Whatever the assessments, one truth remains undeniable: the Cypriot people loved him deeply, and he returned it! Hoping all his life to be worthy of this love. As with so many great men, we only get close to them by discovering their childhoods. He is the one who talks about it best in the magnificent Greek documentary: *H megali Poria*[15]. On August 13, 1913, he was born in the mountain village of Pano Panagia. A hamlet of barely 500 inhabitants to which he will often return to recharge his batteries. His father was a shepherd. He was away for a long time with his goats, far from his family. The little Mikhail[16] preferred, to the dismay of his father hoping for a successor, to help his uncle priest prepare the

---

[15] The Great Epic, from a Greek tv documentary 28.02.2014
[16] His name will be changed to Makarios when he is ordained deacon.

services in the village church. To go to school, he had to cross the Troodos mountains and woods, where he will love walking until the end. Heatwaves in summer, snows in winter, life was tough. During the holidays he helped in the fields as best he could. If you wanted to look for a reason for the melancholy reflection in his large eyes, you would probably find it in the death of his mother, when he was eleven years old. He says he never knew what she died of. Because there was no doctor in the village. One morning she went to bed for a week, before leaving her broken family. His father with three young children will remarry a year later. Makarios says he does not remember when he decided to devote himself to monastic life. But the proximity of the Monastery of the Virgin of Chrysorrogiatissa played a role. His family also often mentioned the name of the famous monastery of the Mother of God of Kykkos. But more powerful than words, it was the campanile that he heard constantly from his village, which attracted the child like a magnet. At the age of thirteen he wanted to enter Kykkos. His father, who was hoping for a shepherd, was not thrilled.

Yet it was he who took his son to the monastery in October 1926. Makarios often wondered "what would his life have been like if he hadn't been to the monastery?"[17] This is indeed where the fate of this village boy was determined, the son of a poor shepherd who could not, when his son was top of the class, pay for his studies. There is always in great destinies a synergy between a desire and the encounters that will allow it to become reality. At the monastery he particularly loved manual work outdoors in the beauty of nature. He learned to forge his soul with the religious services and to exercise the asceticism of patience, so precious for his future life. But the young man dreamed of studying theology. He did think about becoming a hegumen, quickly considering this wish as too lofty. One thing is certain, he claims to have had no wish to enter politics. Even if in 1931, when the English, understanding the strategic interest of the island, were thinking of settling there permanently, the young Makarios wrote on the walls of the monastery: "Long live reunification!" Of course,

---

[17] Ibid. 15

he meant with Greece. The hegumen and the monastery council decided to send the young man to study theology at the University of Nicosia. Aged 20, it is the first time he has been to a big town. Three years of studying in addition to which he reads a lot. In 1936 he was ordained deacon with the name Makarios which means "Blessed". That same year, the monastery allowed him to realise his dream. To study theology and law in Athens. He would say himself that he did not feel disoriented far from his island, on the contrary he was: "A Greek from Cyprus!"[18] It was in Athens in 1940 that the man who always preferred negotiation to force encountered the horror of war. He lived in Athens and got his diploma. At that time he met General Grivas, a Cypriot at the Greek military academy. In 1946 he was ordained a priest, then archimandrite. In the same year, the council of churches sent him to continue studying theology and sociology in Boston. Makarios was not enthusiastic, and the first months in America away from his church were difficult. However, he

---

[18] Ibid. 15

admits to having loved the country and "its democratic spirit, present in all areas of life"[19] by the end of his stay there. In his plans he saw himself as a professor of theology in Athens, but in the middle of his studies a telegram arrived from Cyprus. The people had elected him Metropolitan[20] of Kition, Larnaca district, following in the footsteps of Saint Lazarus. A year after his election he returns to Greece to present the Cypriot problem. But in 1950 his path is once again turned upside down. Archbishop Makarios II dies, and the people elect the shepherd son of Pano Panagia Archbishop of Cyprus, who at age 37 becomes Makarios III. As he likes to recall, the Church of Cyprus is the only one to elect its archbishop with the votes of the clergy and the faithful. This further reinforces the point of fact that the archbishop is welded not only to the spiritual destiny of his people, but also to their ethnic temporal future. His task was heavy and the pitfalls were many: "I heard the Hosanna, but I

---

[19] Ibid. 15
[20] First Bishop

was also crucified!"[21] With sincerity, he adds: "I do not claim that all my actions or all my energies were right, I am a man and am not without fault!"[22] But the love of the Cypriot people was the pillar that carried him through the hardships. At that time the only way to try to get out of the crisis seemed to be that of reuniting with "Mother Greece". A wish for which the Greek people of Cyprus clamoured. Between 1950 and 1955 Makarios travels the world to seek help. But no one wants to offend Britain. He then decides to undertake another, smaller and more solitary, fight. This is the birth of EOKA. Makarios secretly organises General Grivas' return to Cyprus. The English and 18% of the Turks obviously refuse the idea of this reunification. The latter reminding everyone that they are ready to ask Turkey to protect them. In April 1955 the first armed conflicts broke out in Nicosia. English resistance to it was organised. A new government was sent to Cyprus with which Makarios would have many meetings. While Grivas and his troops continued

---

[21] Ibid. 15
[22] Ibid. 15

to plant bombs. On March 8, 1956 Makarios decides to go to Athens, where in the streets the population are demonstrating against British colonisation. On the way to the airport his car is intercepted by the English. He is taken on a plane without knowing where he is headed. From Mombasa he boards a small military boat for an isolated island in the Seychelles. He finds himself cut off from all contact with the outside world. As idyllic as the place might have seemed, he was an exile, a situation that would make him comment that he was "living in a tomb"[23]. But the colonial situation of the English and the French wavers more and more. Since the Suez Crisis of 1956, the international image of the two nations has been damaged. This does not prevent the British from hoping to negotiate with someone other than Makarios, even if it becomes clear that they will not hold on to the colony. The situation is getting worse, freedom is not there. The EOKA fighters must retreat to the mountains. The price is always the same, that of the sacrifice of human life during attacks and

---

[23] Ibid. 15

reprisals. A year after his exile Makarios was released but banned from Cyprus. He goes to Athens where he is welcomed with fervour. From there, still in favour of union with Greece, he goes to plead the case at the United Nations. However, as he explains himself, reality would eventually prevail in favour of the island's total independence. Despite an initial refusal to do so, Makarios would sign the Zürich Agreements in 1959. Infamous rumours circulated about his u-turn. Forced into it by possible British blackmail over his private life. Again, nothing new under the sun! One can wonder however, if the one who insisted on being a man complete with faults and errors, would not have been rubbished well before these agreements. There was no lack among the English, nor among the Turkish Cypriots, nor even among certain envious, disappointed opponents or Greek opponents, of candidates who would have delighted in throwing him to the dogs. To manufacture one of those scandals from which no one emerges victorious! Still, he won the elections brilliantly and on December 13, 1959 became the first president of Cyprus. But, according to the

Agreements, he had to manage his government with a Turkish Cypriot vice-president and a Turkish Cypriot veto in parliament. How did they manage to ignore Byzantine culture and religion, so often oppressed in history by the Ottomans, to hope that such an agreement would settle everything? While Makarios strives to maintain good relations with both Greece and Turkey, the majority of the people are not satisfied. Too many casualties on both sides. Also, to stop the government from sinking, he proposes several amendments to the Zürich Agreements that reduce the rights of the Turkish minority. The Turkish Cypriots resign, vice-president included. As for the Turkish Cypriot population, it exiles itself in the villages and towns inhabited mainly by its own people. Unsurprisingly, each side blames the other for the failure. At the end of 1963, violence resumes between the two communities. We're on the verge of civil war. Without forgetting the basic catalyst, the fact that the signing of the Zürich Agreements had caused disappointment and grudges. In this chaos of fratricidal struggles, Turkey took the opportunity to demand the partition of the island. 1964 Cyprus is on fire and steeped in bloodshed. The Greeks are effecting a rebalancing of power based on demographics. But the Turks, very close to Ankara, are screaming that their security is at stake. The UN then sends in its blue helmets. For its part Greece, after a coup d'état in 1967, falls under the regime of the colonels. In 1968 Makarios is elected by a majority again, even if the ingredients for a tragedy are accumulating. In 1971 Grivas, who had accused Makarios of treason, tries to destabilise him. The second EOKA is formed. But massive demonstrations show that the people are still behind Makarios. However, his national guard is mainly composed of Greeks favourable to Enosis[24]. In 1972 three bishops asked him to forego temporal power. He replaces them and will once again be re-elected by a very large majority in 1973. On January 27, 1974 Grivas succumbs to a heart attack. Although Makarios granted amnesty to his supporters, the guerrillas did not die out. In 1974 the Cypriot National Guard, supported by the

---

[24] Unification of Greece and Cyprus.

Greek colonels, organised a coup against Makarios to join the island with Greece. This one fails, but the excuse is offered on a plate. The Turks of Ankara invade the north of the island. 1600 Greek Cypriots disappear, Turkey has always refused to comment on their fate. Our shepherd's son from Pano Panagia escaped from several attacks during which he was declared dead. He went into temporary exile in Malta and then in London. As for the 38% in the Turkish-occupied north of the island, they will be declared a republic in 1983. But, for flagrant violation of international law, this republic has never been recognised by the rest of the world, Turkey excepted. This is largely due to Makarios' efforts on the international stage during the invasion. In December 1974 the regime of the Greek colonels collapsed. Makarios returns to Cyprus, cheered by the crowds who chant his name. He will assume the presidency until his heart, which he did not take great care of, sounds the end of his epic life. August 3, 1977, a few days before his 64th birthday. His people then parade past continuously to kiss for one last time the hand of the one who had guided, loved and so often blessed them. Representatives from 52 countries are at the funeral. On the route that leads from Nicosia to the tomb he had chosen for himself in Kykkos, where it all began, a weeping human barrier forms on both sides of the road. Throwing flowers and tears on the one that a friend of mine, a Cypriot historian, likes to call "Byzantine prince!"

Other presidents will replace him, but this time it will only be policies. Future archbishops meanwhile, find only their archdiocese.

A reunification project, the Annan plan, was proposed by the UN and put to a referendum of both populations on April 24, 2004 with a view to Cyprus joining the European Union. I was there at the time of the vote and can testify to conversations with the people there, strangers to the complicated developments of these endless treaties. I quote from memory: "on the one hand they had all their property looted in the north of the island, on the other hand they didn't want to see Turkish soldiers parading down their avenues, after the tragedies suffered by so many families". The Turkish North accepts with 65%, while the Greek Cypriots refuse with 76%. So in

2004, only the Greek part entered the European Union. As for Turkey, a possible way into Europe is linked to Ankara's withdrawal from Cyprus. Since then, negotiations have followed one after another, to date without significant success, even if several border posts have been opened since 2005. And a through route to Nicosia in 2008. But increasingly the Turkish authorities are pursuing a policy of active colonisation of the northern part, and many Turkish settlers from Anatolia are settling there. However, I would like to end this overview on a hopeful note. As I relate in the second part of this book, I had the opportunity to talk with the younger generation who did not experience this violence. On both sides, young people are trying to organise peace rallies. May their wishes be granted one day, and prove true to the traditions which shape the soul of the people!

PART TWO

1.

FIRST CONTACT

Kyrie Eleison![25]

Euxaristo[26] and *kalimera*[27] were the only words I knew on my first meeting with Cyprus.

27 years ago...

This story begins at some 11,000 metres above sea level. After two years of pandemic exile, I finally find myself on a plane bound for this big rock lost between the East and the West. Traveling in October 2021 is like an obstacle course. Despite a carcass that really does not need

---

[25] Lord have mercy!
[26] Thank you
[27] Hello

to rub up against this "Minus"[28] demon, I could not resist! *It was a long road, but I made the road, the one that led to you, and I am not perjured, if this evening I swear to you, that for you, I would have done it on my knees...*[29] Yes, it is indeed a love story! It didn't start with love at first sight, far from it! In the 90s we spent a week in an infrastructure that could not have been more touristy. The famous flight/hotel/pick-up from the airport formula. The trip had started badly with a long delay, a British plane finally replacing that of the Cypriot company. It was April. We had just celebrated Easter in the Orthodox Church of France to which I will always be grateful for having welcomed me without reservation, into a universe of infinite treasures, the richness of which I could not have conceived beforehand. Bathed in our Easter euphoria, we were hardly inclined to embed still further a tradition that we considered too Eastern. Suspecting its name complicit with a form of obscurantism, expressing itself moreover in an archaic language,

---

[28] This is the name the author gives to the Covid-19 virus in her book *The Tenth Plague* (Huge Jam Publishing, 2021).
[29] My most beautiful love story, *Barbara's Song.*

with songs which seemed to us soporific in their monotony. It is strange how as people we are used to missing out on so many treasures, locked up in our comforting prejudices.

A night-time arrival, my first memory of waking up to a cheek decorated with mosquito bites is the only one that stayed with me. The few steps around a hotel complex on the outskirts of Larnaca, left little more impression on me than any touristic concrete surrounded by Mediterranean palm trees. Despite a cold wind, I took my first communion with the Cypriot sea. After lunch we walked to Larnaca to enter a ghost town. Everything was closed. We then realised that it was their Good Friday[30] which at that time made no concessions to the tourist economy. With some annoyance at a tradition unable to celebrate Holy Week on a civilised date[31], we decided to visit Saint Lazarus Cathedral. We weren't the only ones. Not that other tourists had got lost, but we found ourselves in a long line of Greek Cypriots, waiting in the Eastern style. As

---

[30] Holy Friday
[31] The West celebrates Holy Week on a different date from Orthodox Christians.

is the custom on Good Friday, the epitaphion[32] had been placed in a magnificent tomb decorated with white flowers. The Orthodox come to prostrate themselves before the Son of God, to embrace him and to venerate him. From this episode I retained that perfume of flowers, incense and rose water which was beginning to impose itself as one of the seals of an Orient I knew nothing about.

On Saturday in the middle of the night we were awakened by an earthquake of explosions. Larnaca vibrated to us, with that vibration that will continue to resound, like that of the Resurrection. Indeed, the hotel receptionist will confirm that what had disturbed our sleep was none other than this "cry" of all the Orthodox on Easter night: *"Xristos anesti!"*[33]

The next day we rented a car to visit Nicosia. Clinging to the steering wheel with concentration, because a former British colony obliges us to drive on the left! We parked the car without difficulty just on the side of St. John's

---

[32] An ornate embroidered sheet representing Christ laying in His tomb.
[33] Christ is risen!

Cathedral, which in today's Nicosia is an impossible feat! Nicosia was not yet more of a European capital than any European capital. With a tragic peculiarity, however, that of a demarcation line still trembling from a recent conflict, dividing the city between Greek Cypriots and Turkish Cypriots. Sandbags piled up in the exposed passageways, with soldiers on both sides who this time were not guarding the tomb of Christ. The presence of UN soldiers, ignoring the dramas it had caused, seemed to us a palpable tension. On the way back we turned on the radio and came across Radio Kiti.[34] It was broadcasting songs of the Resurrection. Different from our Gregorian tones, pouring out joy at the top of their voices, these were a combination of serene jubilation and angelic beauty. We stopped the car to listen. I was then literally overwhelmed by an emotion that escaped me, and which I perceived had overwhelmed many others centuries before me...

It was my first experience of being dazzled by a tradition that my fiercely independent will and

---

[34] Kition is the ancient name for Larnaca.

my ignorance had relegated to the box of archaisms!

2.

INSPIRED INTUITION

Yet our desires went to new horizons, Greece and Crete. We discovered Crete with our well-established off-circuit formula. Two backpacks, a mini tent that opened like an umbrella, two mattresses and two light duvets. Car rental at the airport and camping. Accustomed to camping since childhood, this formula suited me perfectly. Crete seduced us and we had planned to return.

In 1998 we already had our tickets for Heraklion. Without sounding like an illuminati, I am convinced that, although we imagine ourselves very free, sometimes "fate" gives us a little boost! Of course, we have the freedom to accept it or reject it. It was August 15th, feast of the Dormition of the Mother of God, which is the feast of my name. Mireille, from the Hebrew Myriam meaning Mary. While incensing the icon of the Virgin, Pierre felt one of those callings from within: "Leave for Cyprus!" We then decided to go into exile. With the desire this time to get closer to the Orthodox tradition of this unknown East. A few days later Pierre went to change our tickets. We boarded a Cyprus Airways plane on the evening of September 13th, in readiness for our project. In the middle of the night a taxi dropped us in front of the only campsite in the Larnaca district, just beyond the hotel complex from our first trip. I see myself at the entrance to this forest of parched eucalyptus, with backpacks our only companions. I was 48 and for the first time I felt a pain in my right hip…

The unlit campsite was empty. We opened our umbrella as close to the beach as possible. Installation by torchlight, followed by a dip in the sea which resembled a heated bathtub. Old women sitting on the sand took advantage of the absence of the sun. Cypriots are hospitable and very curious. With our slightly enriched vocabulary, especially Pierre's, we answered the usual round of questioning. When we mentioned the Feast of the Exaltation of the Cross, what happened was what would happen so many times. A display of wonder in the face of French Orthodox. Hospitality deviates towards an apparent complicity after that.

When the manager of the place woke up, a Greek came to collect the modest sum for our pitch. He gave us the key to a cabin with a single tap to wash everything there was to wash! We realised for the first time that in Cyprus, water is such a rare and capricious gift. Drinkable water, you have to buy in a bottle. In three weeks I took only one shower, almost embarrassed to waste it, in a barracks where I had to plead Open Sesame even while the sea was just a stone's throw away.

We had only two neighbours, two friendly Swiss guys living between an apartment at a congested crossroads and their caravan at the campsite. They had abandoned their small business in the Grisons to wait for their pensions in Larnaca. Mr. worked nights in a hotel and

Mrs. cleaned the campsite toilets. And no, the Swiss are not all rich bankers! The organisation of our daily life was spartan. Just the journeys without a car were an epic. On foot in approaching 40-degree heat, or by bus with our first friendly Cypriot experience. The driver, no doubt moved by our tenacity in using the local public transport, as well as by our persistence in speaking Greek rather than English, invited us to drink coffee at the terminal. After this baptism at the corner of a table on a potholed pavement, he gave us the wink to put away our ticket money, as we wanted to pay, inviting us to sit down at the community's expense! We had recovered old boxes for our meals in front of the tent, as well as an old sofa for a nap in the shade. On weekends, the few empty caravans filled up. The whispering of the waves then gave way to the laughter of happy bands. A Cypriot is never alone. But it only takes two Cypriots to make a lot of noise. However, it's not the noise of the smartphone, but the noise of life. The life we love to share. Because in Cyprus we love life and we let it be known!

On the first Sunday, we wanted to go to the

liturgy. Scorched crossing of burned fields to get to the nearest village church. Decked out in my only appropriate outfit, a wrinkled orange skirt, an orange strappy top, shoulders covered by an equally orange shawl, I had to look like a lost gypsy in the midst of the people of God in their Sunday Best. In truth I was! Gypsy, looking for I knew not what on the roads, and lost, because what I was looking for had not yet found a name. We were welcomed with trusting hospitality and took communion after a liturgy that seemed to me to be endless. I only took in the service thanks to the rites, recognising only my famous Kyrie Eleison, Amen and Hallelujah! Which – by the way – is the main thing! This was my first contact with the Greek Orthodox liturgy…

At the campsite we had a company of half-wild cats. According to tradition, they were brought to the island by Saint Helena. When she stopped over in Cyprus on the way from Jerusalem, after the discovery of the Holy Cross. There she also founded the monastery of Stravrovouni, which means the mountain of the cross, where she left a piece of the precious wood. A monastery reserved only for men, on top of a hill overlooking the plain of Larnaca. We went up there one day and had a prayer in the chapel in front of the monastery. It was from this blessed belvedere that we contemplated, for the first time, that expanse so withered by the Cypriot sun. Already at that time allergic to heatwaves, I nevertheless always had a weakness for deserts. I felt this one even more intensely, a piece of the holy cross a few metres behind me. A presentiment of the crosses that were in store for me?

3.

PREPARATIONS

Before returning, we had to find a rental for the following year. I had quit my job, and Pierre was responsible for some of his family. Therefore we looked for a modestly-priced neighbourhood. Driven to town by our driver friend, we walked along the sea towards an old quarter of the small fishing port. Next to old houses, there were high concrete buildings, and we stopped in front of the door of one of them that had an inscription in English "House of God". I remember joking, "This is where we're headed!" On the way back we went to the covered market to buy those succulent Cypriot grapes. The stallholder who spoke perfect French ended up offering to rent her apartment to us. Deal concluded with the first rent's deposit.

Back in France we piled up our furniture, at the time not yet scattered by many moves, in an old apartment in Bordeaux. Gypsies but not unconsciously so, we wanted to keep a base. And we enrolled at the university for modern Greek courses…

We had planned to go by boat with our car, backpacks being a bit restrictive for a whole year's luggage. In the boot we placed our camping gear, in order to explore the island before settling in Larnaca.

June 1999, here we are on the road, ready to enter the third millennium on this big rock lost between East and West…

4.

THE TRIP

We found ourselves in the port of Ancona with Albanian truck drivers. I chatted with one of them who moved me, because while waiting to board, he was learning languages in his truck. Our little Volkswagen in the hold, we still had to find two seats on a Greek ship, liaising between Ancona and Patras for a journey of about two days. Unable to sleep sitting up, I unrolled my mattress and sleeping bag to settle on the floor. I was 49 years old and felt as light as when, hair woven with flowers, I was acting the hippie on the paths of Asia.

Having landed in Patras, our first stop was the

cathedral with its tomb and the relics of Saint Andrew. Andrea being my middle name and the name of my beloved grandfather.[35] The relics were unfamiliar to us, even a little suspicious. What good was it to worship and kiss bones? Under the gaze of the Mother of God in the dome, I was introduced to this tradition, the meaning of which I would only later understand. Without thinking, I let myself be drawn into this sacred atmosphere. And I laid my forehead on that of the first-called, Andrew's. Tired from the trip, I then took a dip in the sea, then we went to a campsite near Epidaurus. Four days before the next boat from Piraeus to Limassol. After boarding we joined the vagabonds on deck for an unforgettable journey. The open air and the sea, with only the waves and the sky as the horizon, filled a need in me. Before leaving Piraeus, we joined the passengers who were gazing at Athens. A group of Greek Roman Catholics were singing Vespers, to begin the pilgrimage that would take them to Israel. We made friends with their adorable priest, originally from Patras. He spoke

---

[35] From where the pen name Maria Andreas comes.

French admirably and became a friend. On deck, our companions were all figures that I cannot help describing. Two gorgeous Swedish girls, young students out and about. A Swiss disguised in a traditional Appenzell costume, a loner who spoke only with his black Labrador. Too bad, I would have liked to know what had led him to this bridge, without ever foregoing his national dress. Next to us we had a young, touchingly beautiful Israeli couple. They were returning home, the ship continuing to Haifa. We discussed the hopes they had of their new prime minister. The hopes of young people are similar and often noble. At dawn when the wind was blowing, Pierre had covered them with his sleeping bag while they slept. Which earned us a share of delicious coffee, prepared on their little stove. Finally, a German, whose confidante I quickly became. He had lost his job, his wife had left him, and although his mother had threatened to kill herself if he left, he had resolved to set off at random. Assaulted, injured and robbed at night in the port of Piraeus, he had been treated in ER. As soon as a new bank card arrived, he got on the first boat. Equipped with what he had on his back and a course of antibiotics to prevent infection of his wounds. As food, or rather as drink, he sipped retsina, that famous Greek white wine. Obviously the retsina and the antibiotics did not mix well, because he fell victim to a sordid diarrhoea. He wasn't discouraged though. I will never forget the comic spectacle of our chap in a long, soaked T-shirt, wringing out his jeans behind his back, while trying to impress one of the two Swedes. So much for our fellow travellers. Perhaps our trip would not have been so unique in first class!

We made a first stopover in Rhodes, not yet invaded in June 1999. Then continued at night, the "long road that led to you"[36]. In the early morning we were awakened by the boat's siren. A thick mist veiled the landscape. Suddenly, like in one of those terrifying Scottish tales, it appeared to us like a fortified castle awash in mystery. The Monastery of Saint John the Theologian. While our German friend went in search of retsina, we climbed the path that led to the cave, where the exiled St. John had received

---

[36] Ibid. 29

the Revelation. Not caring much about the back pain I was used to, I had put on a corset I had worn for years as a teacher. Once again I felt light...or almost! Blessed times because world tourism was not yet crowded into buses. We were able to calmly let ourselves be penetrated by every detail of this sanctuary. The trace in the rock where Saint John had laid his head all his nights in exile, brought me tears of communion. With the one I continue to implore every morning, to allow me to make this trip again, by plane this time. The atheists will smile, and I understand, but I have learned since my meeting in Patras and another in Patmos, that pilgrimages establish an intimacy with the saint who is venerated there. A privilege for which I will be eternally grateful...

5.

ARRIVAL IN LIMASSOL

The advantage of the boat is that we have time to savour. We walked along that big rock to Limassol. Formalities upon docking are protracted, with Cyprus not yet being in Europe. Then we headed towards Paphos via the only four routes that cross the island. The landscape did not really differ from any Mediterranean landscape, but was already suffocating in the summer oven. I looked at Pierre, who seemed rather attracted by the green forests, and I said to myself: "It's off to a bad start!" In Paphos, the campsite listed in the travel guide looked nothing like a campsite. So we continued towards Polis.

A eucalyptus wood in which we were again the only customers. A first meal next to our tent with halloumi[37], bread, tomatoes and grapes. A sunny repast, of the sun, of the sun we gorged upon! After a few days in the charming town of Polis, we went to Larnaca to check on our apartment. Bad surprise, the lady had found a more lucrative tenant. We could hardly see ourselves spending a year beneath our big umbrella. So we strolled randomly through the old quarter that we already knew. Coincidence? At the corner of a garden that was not a garden, behind a wall between two buildings bordering a badly paved and dusty road, a giant was cutting down what was left of his hedge of withered jasmines. Hearing us speak, he addressed us in impeccable French. A Lebanese Palestinian, he had studied in France for a long time. He told us about the caretaker of a nearby building who could tell us if there were any vacant apartments. We rented a studio-flat on the spot from the young Cypriot. Guess where? Just above the inscription: "House of God!" We have changed apartments several

---

[37] This cheese originates from Cyprus.

times, but for 20 years, we have not left this neighbourhood of which I know every corner. The rent for the studio was 90 Cypriot liras, which today amounts to around 160 euros per month. It certainly wasn't luxury: two spartan beds, a kitchenette, a small balcony, a table and two plastic chairs. No air conditioning but a bathtub all to ourselves! Returning to Polis, we went the next day to the liturgy of Saint Peter and Saint Paul. The priest we chatted with had eyes that were huge and, unusually for a Cypriot, as blue as the sky. Not the shadow of a cloud either in this man of a beauty as modest as it was lordly. On the 30th, the Feast of the Holy Apostles, we undertook to bleach what was to be our new home. Luckily there was no water shortage that day! This was to happen many times, when the boats bringing water from Crete were late. Since then, sea desalination plants have been built. But the water thus obtained is much more expensive for Cypriots, so I beg our tourist friends not to take four showers a day!

6.

FIRST FRIENDS

At the beginning of July our new life began.

The Palestinian giant and his wife were happy to give us advice. He had, like so many others, been expelled with his family from Haifa[38]. He had still been a child, but he remembered carrying his little brother in his arms. A refugee in Lebanon, he had acquired a foothold in Larnaca during the conflicts that shook this country he loved. He had just retired from being a UN employee. Intelligent, cultured, he was fluent in French and English alongside Arabic. It

---

[38] Port town in the north of Israel.

was a real history lesson to listen to him talk about his experiences, enriched by his great knowledge of the Middle East. One of his behavioural analyses struck me. He said that in Judeo-Christian mentalities, even among non-practicing people, when you shook hands for a contract knowing that you had fooled the other, you felt a form of guilt. Whereas in other cultures, it was something to be proud about. Without any moral judgement, it would sometimes be good to know the educated-thus-through-the-centuries subconscious better! As for his "prophecies" on his dear Lebanon, they have unfortunately all come true. At the age of 20 he jumped on a bomb and had his leg and two fingers amputated. I have never known a disabled person so at ease – if I may say so – with their disability. Impossible to forget his powerful laugh, a permanent snub to the ordeal. His wife, a charming little woman, a maths professor, was a curious mixture of finesse, intelligence and childish naivety. She loved to tell us about her village in the Lebanese mountains and her pilgrimages to Saint Charbel[39]. But also of her life as a teacher during the conflicts. When everyone had to throw themselves under the tables to protect themselves from shots and bombs. How many evenings have we spent, seated in this garden that isn't one, behind a wall between two buildings bordering a badly paved and dusty road? We do not count the nights of lightness, laughter and shadowless exchanges, because we think they will be eternal! In 2000 they belatedly became parents to twins. Since then, the giant has been obsessed with providing his children with the best education. After many attempts to return to Lebanon, one of which resulted in an emergency flight during the last conflict, the giant decided to leave for the USA. I remember this sad confession: "My father jumped on a bomb, I jumped on a bomb, I don't want my son to jump on a bomb!" Today the twins are at the University of Los Angeles, but the parents aspire to come to grow old in Larnaca. How I understand them! Yet the climate is harsh for those who are not used to it.

---

[39] Lebanese hermit priest monk, 1828-1898

Hot in summer, sometimes icy and humid in winter, windy and often dusty. Larnaca constantly turns its gaze to the sky, imploring the rain! That famous summer of 1999, how many times did we spend part of our evenings in the bathtub, when there was water? Or go to the seaside in the middle of the night, to try to cool off? Getting up very early, I went swimming with the Cypriots before the tourists took to the beach to grill themselves. I then went home to work on my distance-learning psychology courses, while Pierre slumped on the bed, blinds closed, studying Greek. The building opposite in the evening reflected the accumulated heat back to us, and we were in a permanent oven.

7.

THE CYPRIOT FAMILY FROM ABOVE

As we stopped at the side of a road in search of a bookshop, I had no idea that that morning in July 1999 would bring my heart many upheavals.

After addressing two priests in English, the younger invited us to the liturgy in a jewel of a Byzantine chapel. The elder, rector of the parish and renowned theologian, welcomed us with generosity. He introduced us to the community with that confident simplicity that characterises men of prayer: "Maria and Pierre, two French people. They were on the road and now they are here!" This was our first community anchor. We spent our Sundays there as well as the liturgical feast days, or fêtes. After the liturgy we were invited to the parish centre for typical Cypriot breakfasts, as copious as they are succulent. On Saturday evening after vespers, we stayed for a brief theological talk with our rector, now a friend. I only understood a few rare words, but I felt the fluid of life.

Of Life…

We also laughed a lot, shared words, sang. Even danced! More specifically, Pierre danced, on this bright 2001 Easter Monday, when he joined the circle of the faithful for those famous Greek dances that accompany the sound of sunny melodies. It was cheerful, it was light. Of that lightness that caresses the soul.

Despite the memory of my body aching during those long services, they gradually imposed themselves as an essential rendezvous. First with the richness of the Greek language, which the rest of my life will not be enough to explore. Then with the so-called Byzantine tradition, inseparable from this language. The

Logos[40] then began to unveil a face. His face. His eyes that told me that He really was Alpha and Omega. I must immediately make it clear that I have not become a better person for it, but I have acquired this privilege of accepting that my mediocrity is unique. And that He is tirelessly ready to welcome it...

Immersed in this universe, I started to take a different look at the icons. Or rather it was they who, step by step, came to me. Like an immense family populated by saints, martyrs, scenes whose intensity of encounter go beyond the most wise theological discourse. I will never forget that night of August 14th, the eve of the Dormition of the Mother of God. The small chapel being crowded, I had taken refuge on a stool outside, facing the large icon of the Dormition of Mary. Once again my perspiring body was suffocating. I then clung to my patron saint lying there, surrounded by the gathered apostles. In front of her body which had engendered the God-Man, holding in his arms a swaddled baby[41], Christ

---

[40] With a small 'l' this means 'the word' in Greek; with a capital 'L' it means Christ.
[41] Traditionally, this swaddled baby represents Mary's soul.

had come to welcome the soul of his mother. This scene emanated such calm that for the first time, death seemed sweet to me. Like a light leap, during which it would suffice to entrust oneself to the arms of the One who had vanquished it by his Resurrection. Ever since, I continue to place my hand in Saint Lazarus's on the great icon of his cathedral. In tears I lay my forehead on the Virgin's mantle in my monastery. Or I converse eye to eye with one of the many saints that I like to count, even if they lived elsewhere, among the members of my Cypriot family "from above". The atheists will smile, and I was enough of one in my time to understand them! But at no time have I regretted adopting and being adopted by this family, painted by laypeople or monks in a communion that transpires still. Even in the icy winter winds!

8.

FIRST STEPS IN THE TROODOS

After the agape[42] of August 15th, I collapsed on my bed like a sleepwalker. In the heart of summer the oven had become unbearable. So we took out our big umbrella and fled to the Troodos. On the mountain range that crosses the centre of the island and whose summit flirts with a height of 2000 metres.

Along the way, we branched off onto a road that leads to one of the many monasteries of the Mother of God. But the festivities had drawn a

---

[42] The food we share after the liturgy.

crowd of Cypriots, and the cars were parked higgledy-piggledy on the sides of the mountain. So we turned back. Little did I know, lost in the middle of nowhere, that this road would become My Road! The one I would take and retake and take again. The one that I would dream of taking again, the moment I left it...

At that time there was only one campsite, located just on from the hamlet of Prodromos. The sleepy campsite was packed. We were barely able to plant our umbrella facing the top. As soon as the sun went down, we went around the place which suddenly came alive, like a fair in the middle of chimes. Families, friends who loved to share in the same activities, ate meat that had been grilled on the charcoal. As I said before, rarely is a Cypriot alone! We wandered a little, lost in the middle of the songs, the smoke of the grills and the laughter. Because in Cyprus we like to laugh and we let it be known! It was a little drunk that we went to bed in a coolness that seemed to come straight from paradise. The problem was that we only had our summer clothes and two red nylon jackets worn around the world. But, if the days are torrid, Troodos nights at this altitude are icy. Shivering, we covered ourselves with everything we could find, bath towels and boxes included! Awakened by the cold in the middle of the night, I left the tent. I was then transported to the kingdom of the fairies. An enchanting Troodos night that resembled tales from my childhood. I sat facing the mountain and held my breath in front of the Universe. Unique Troodos night. Night so dense, and yet I had never been so close to golden light. The gold of light. Simply gold! The stars were people. They smiled in a world still more or less in order. They were smiling at me. The heatwave, the crushing road, the sickening smoke, evaporated as, vibrating with a sacred melody, the night waved its wand. The crowning glory of pure beauty! Suddenly a small, bright white owl came out to hunt. She was circling in front of me, and I wanted to believe she was asking me to dance. It was one of the most intense nights of my life, a night of reunion with all forms of communion in unison!

9.

FIRST ANGELIC ENCOUNTER

We got up early, before the sun hit us. After a frugal breakfast, we packed a no less frugal picnic and set off for the mountains along a stream, until the cool of the evening. We met not a single living soul. One morning we decided to take the road back to the monastery. We crossed the thirsty pine forest again, to finally see, in the nook of the mountain, this monastery that would very quickly invite itself into the nook of my heart, into the nook of my love.

In the yard, a huge oak tree that would become the symbol of my tenacity to come back again and again. We entered the great Church of the Mother of God, and for the first time there I venerated and kissed the icon of my patron saint. We were still alone at this privileged time, with no influx of pilgrims. Savouring body and soul the silence and the presence of the visible and invisible world. Coming out into the inner courtyard, we were approached by a tiny monk, who asked us where we were from. I was immediately dazzled by his gaze. "A look darker than night and brighter than the sun. I had never seen eyes so beautiful, so big. So flamboyant. So overflowing with Love…"[43] When he heard the name of France, he began to recite like a child his memories of school that he would remind us of each visit: *"cuisinier-cuisinière, jardinier-jardinière, écolier-écolière…"* I like to imagine the kid with the huge black eyes, repeating the grammar rhymes like this, he who was destined to become an angel! Before taking leave, he wanted to know our first names to put them in his prayers. I'm sure they carried us and continue to carry us, wherever he is! In October, when we returned to

---

[43] *Hook Up with Your Angel* Maria Andreas (Huge Jam Publishing, 2022)

the monastery, it was again he who invited us, since we were Orthodox, to come and attend vespers in their little chapel. A few years later, when we had become familiar, he asked us after vespers to accompany him to their chapel of Saint Neophytos[44], to light the night lights there. He added with a smile that belonged only to him: "because we have been friends for years!" When we arrived in front of the icons, he handed me the little flame: "It's Maria who will light the night lights!" Today this mundane gesture appears to me as a blessed symbol. To receive in my unworthy hand, I say that without false humility, the flame of an angel! This friendship grew stronger, and with each visit, it seemed as if we had left each other the day before. Illness did not spare him. First an operation for stomach cancer, after which the doctors gave him six months to live. However, while of course the sick are permitted to take a less stringent approach to dietary asceticism, he refused the chicken broth diet, continuing to take his monk's food. And this for many years after the fatal diagnosis! It was

---

[44] Saint Neophytos was a Cypriot recluse (1134-1215).

he too who made me understand the grace of the monastic vow of obedience. One day when the three of us were in the yard, I asked him if I could take a picture. He replied: "yes, but I have to ask permission from the gerondas."[45] He said that with such simplicity, such accuracy, that I wasn't even surprised. Even more, I realised how we were constantly torn in all directions, imbued with our so-called freedom. While this little fragment of angel was content to perform the tasks of community life by relying on the decisions of the one he had chosen. To judge what would hurt his soul, or simply distract him from prayer. The one that multiplied the stars in his eyes. I forwent my photo, preferring to enjoy every second of his presence. Today I regret it a little, even if his big black eyes can never be erased from my memory. One evening, he explained to us that his heart was sick, and that he had just been offered a heart transplant in Germany. A proposal that he refused, because he confided to us: "I want to continue to pray with my own heart, until the end!" More and more I

---

[45] The higoumen that the monks choose to lead them.

got into the habit of going to the monastery alone, Pierre being busy with his parish. Each time, he had a few words in French and spoke them with childlike candour. Or he would come to remind me of the time of the next service or to talk to me about a saint. Little by little the pilgrims flocked in. As soon as a bus arrived, he would rush, equipped with a bucket and a broom, towards the monastery's public toilets to clean them. In the chapel, to which he had invited us in October 1999, and which has become my chapel of intimacy with God and my brother monks, he opened and closed the curtain of the sanctuary each time the priest passed. Or he was ahead of him with a lighted candle. A light bearing The Light! It was there that I saw him for the last time, 20 years after our first meeting. After offices, as I worshipped the iconostasis[46], he approached with that step I would recognise among millions. Discreet and light, like the rustle of angelic wings. And this human bundle of prayer, out of breath with his tired heart, whispered to me with a sacred elfin

---

[46] An icon-covered partition separating the nave from the sanctuary.

smile: "A few days ago, my Noùs[47] told me that presbytera[48] Maria was coming to the monastery, and now you are here!" I believe that I have never received a more precious declaration of Love! When I think of that moment, tears of gratitude well up in my eyes. A few months later, the stroke that struck him ended up winning. The hieromonk who was with him in Nicosia told me that he had not even noticed the moment of his departure: "Just a peaceful illumination. That of purity". I cried. For the first time since my brother died, I mourned a member of my family. I went to his tomb under the pines and I placed some seashells there. I knew right away, despite his being in our own prayers for our deceased, that he's the one praying for us now. So thank you petit angel! Treasure of my impure heart! I know I was never worthy to meet your fiery gaze. May it help me burn off some of my unworthiness...

---

[47] Untranslatable in French too, this can be described as the soul's eye.
[48] The Greek name given to priests' wives.

10.

UPHEAVALS

On the third Sunday of August, the holidays being over, the campsite emptied. There were only three of us left, the two of us and the little owl. At the end of the month, hoping that the hot weather would have passed, we went back down. We understood that September would not be less torrid on the plains, and we decided to accept it. Life in the studio flat resumed, and we found out more about the people around us. First, a solitary eccentric who walked his two dogs and his cat every morning. He always had an anecdote about his trio, his only family. Then the prostitute on the ground floor opposite who, singing and dancing, opened her windows every Saturday evening. The cries of the neighbour upstairs never interrupted her. That neighbour having other grievances besides the music, because her husband seemed to stop off at the singer's place rather often. They were an Austrian couple who lived there year-round. They had a common passion, cats, which were not lacking in Larnacan streets at that time. Whatever the temperature, they left for the butcher's around noon to pick up the offcuts. They came back sweating, encumbered with sacks of equally sweaty meat. Madame did the cooking, then Monsieur distributed the meals to about forty cats who came running to his call. They too had their musical ritual. Every Friday between 9:00 p.m. and 1:00 a.m., they offered us a session of Strauss waltzes at full decibels. Alas Strauss was not alone. The couple took the opportunity to settle their accounts. First loudly, then very loudly, and finally screaming. At that stage, Monsieur would begin to repeat a single sentence, dozens of times at that: "Ich auch!"[49]

---

[49] Me too!

So much so that we baptised him: "Ich auch!" I sometimes wonder what has become of "Ich auch", the benefactor of cats. In this district, at the time a place for discreet meetings of the pleasures of the flesh, the same customers often made rounds with their vans. Our studio flat had probably housed a lady of the night. One evening when Pierre was in town, someone called round and I went to the door. A Cypriot who had already unbuttoned his trousers exclaimed: "But this isn't Eva!" I retorted: "No it isn't Eva, it's Maria!" Either I was not to his liking, or Maria doesn't suit as a prostitute's first name, because the gentleman quickly left. Since then, prostitutes, especially foreign ones, creep around Saint Lazarus cathedral. A story as old as time itself...

We didn't have a phone, and it was from a dilapidated phone box that we called our parents every week. One day in this overheated box I learned that my father, in the midst of a crisis over a herniated disc, had been hospitalised. The situation becoming critical, we decided that I would make the trip. I left for six weeks and I realise today that Pierre was left alone. I am infinitely grateful to him! I remember the plane flying over Cape Kiti, from where he told me he would come to say goodbye. My mission was exhausting, his ascetic. He took the opportunity to stay at Stravrovouni, the monastery reserved for men. When I came back, October was still one of those Octobers of yesteryear, mild and pleasant. And I was determined to continue my conquest of Cypriot culture…

11.

A BLESSED NEW ENCOUNTER

With the end of summer signalling the start of activities, we enrolled in Greek courses, as well as iconography courses offered by the district of Larnaca. If we were only foreigners on the Greek course, we were the only two "barbarians" on the iconography course. The teacher called the register at the beginning of each lesson. When it came to our name, he smiled: "Oi dio Galloi!"[50] While Pierre got off to a most honourable start, I was never able to finish the nose of the infant Jesus who was being held by the Virgin, despite

---

[50] The two French people!

the wise corrections of our teacher. But I remember the magnificent slides he showed us of frescoes and icons. Little by little our Greek was improving, and we could not resist participating in a conference on Saint Gregory Palamas, organised by the district of Limassol. I took out my beautiful black dress, and we bought an equally beautiful black jacket for Pierre, who had neither displayed his cassock nor his priesthood, since the canonical troubles of the ECOF[51]. We took a room in a small hotel in Limassol, which was not yet the conquered territory of Russian billionaires. And here we were ready to plunge, black robed and black jacketed, into a crowd of bishops, monks, priests, psychiatrists and lay-people from all over the world. It was there that we met for the first time the child of the country, the hegumen Ephraim of Vatopédi.[52] The conference took place in a large hotel by the sea. From afar we had seen our two priest friends from Larnaca along with the Archimandrite of Saint Lazarus Cathedral. We didn't know anyone else. When the lectures started, we

---

[51] Catholic Orthodox Church of France
[52] Mount Athos Monastery, Greece

realised how much of our Greek was still of neophyte standard. Frankly, we only understood the ones given in English. So we welcomed the breaks with relief, especially since there was an abundance of drinks and delicious petit fours on offer. Sometimes Pierre took the opportunity to relax and make me laugh. He paced the reception hall shouting in front of him: "Eimaste Galloi!"[53] You guess right, we did not meet other Gauls! On the other hand, during one of these refreshment breaks, I was going to meet someone who marked my soul deeply. I saw in the crowd a lonely little cleric with a very long and beautiful beard. He stood discreetly in a corner, carrying an antique briefcase under his arm. Even today I don't know why, but I went straight to him and asked him in English if I hadn't already seen him at the Saint Serge Institute[54] in Paris. He replied in French: "No, but the best book on theology I have ever read was written in French by Vladimir Lossky."[55] It was the book: *Essay on the Mystical*

---

[53] We are French!
[54] Institute of Orthodox Theology
[55] Russian Orthodox theologian born in 1903 in Göttingen, dying in 1958 in Paris.

Theology of the Eastern Church.[56] It could not have been better, I had found studying this difficult text intensely challenging! I told him, and we chatted a bit. Before returning to the conference room, he said to me: "Come and see me at Larnaca Metropol, I work there, and my church is not far." At that moment I didn't know the hours I was about to spend in the next 20 years, either in that large office still open in Larnaca's Metropol, or in one of the most beautiful churches in Larnaca. They were among the richest of my spiritual quest. In the presence not only of a historian, but a theologian too, I never experienced the embarrassment of a teaching too convoluted, but always presented in a clear and embodied language. He had two funny mannerisms that I remember fondly. The first, which he described as a "passion", was gorging himself in the summer on ice cubes taken from the fridge. The second, that of pushing a pen in his ear to scratch vigorously. I was always afraid that he would puncture his eardrum! But that did not prevent me from deepening with him the

---

[56] Éditions du Cerf (French publishing house)

tradition of penance. The one that corrects the egocentrism of the heart and heals it thanks to the mercy of God.[57] He also enlightened me on many historical aspects of this big pebble[58] which took an increasingly central place in my life. So, regardless of the heatwave, I'm left with nothing but gratitude!

---

[57] These themes are developed in more detail in Maria Andreas' book *La Mort n'a pas Dieu* (Amazon 2017).

[58] The author explains her metaphor thus: i) travelling there in late September the view out the window on landing was burnt like a stone and every time I thought,'my beloved, so beloved, big burnt pebble' ii) I love pebbles on the beach, rolling for centuries... iii) it's a kind of reminder that it is small, humble, lost in the sea...

12.

PREMATURE RETURN

I had known for a long time that my back was in bad shape and no longer reacted much to its regular torments. However, one evening – I remember the date, it was November 27th – we decided to go to vespers at Saint Lazarus on foot. One of those mercilessly icy winds from the Mediterranean began to blow. Suddenly I felt such pain in my leg that I couldn't move forward. I knew that if my leg was affected, it could become critical, and I panicked. Pierre went to get the car. Then began a series of examinations. As a neurologist claimed that it wasn't stemming from the back, we did not know what to think. So I decided to move as little as possible and remained lying on my bed, facing an old gas stove. I left Pierre alone to continue the Greek and iconography lessons. Often in the evening, while preparing the meal before he came home, I would look out the window at the icy December fog and question aloud: "Maria, what are you looking for?"

It was lying on those uncomfortable beds, opposite a first-generation TV set and a pre-war stove, that we crossed the threshold of the third millennium! One night I was seized with a crisis of tachycardia strong enough for Pierre to wrap me in a blanket and drive me to ER. He put me in a wheelchair and rushed in, shouting, "*Kardia, Kardia!*" I was well cared for, but after that incident we decided to turn off the medieval stove. This meant that we slept wrapped up in our winter clothes, scarves and hats included. It really wasn't such a sad sight! Especially for someone who did not really know what she was looking for! Around January 10th we resolved to return. Impossible to contemplate the trip by car. It therefore stayed in Larnaca, while we took the plane. I felt immense sadness, despite the heatwaves, the freezing winds, then anxiety, when the plane took off, taking me to a series of medical visits that I describe in my book: *Illness, My Complicit Enemy.*[59]

It wasn't my back at that point, but my totally worn-out hip that caused me at 49 to walk around for three years with two crutches.

I had not forgotten my big pebble and had only one desire, to show it to my crutches. It was I who maintained contact by letter with our Cypriot friends, with the hope of returning there as soon as possible. As for Pierre, he contented himself with taking a flight in February and valiantly returning the car in record time!

---

[59] Maria Andreas (Amazon 2021)

13.

THE CYPRIOT FAMILY FROM BELOW

Armed with my crutches, I accompanied Pierre to the University of Bordeaux for modern Greek lessons with a brilliant teacher. In March 2001, we are finally in Piraeus again, waiting to board for my island. Rehoused in the same building, right next to our Palestinian friends, but with air conditioning!

Once again greeted with warm hospitality, we joined the new church to which our young priest friend had been assigned. Little by little we were adopted by its typically Cypriot family. I was lucky enough to meet the widowed grandfather, a former tailor who had been employed by the English. I knew that his life was hard, that he made clothes for the faithful at the Easter liturgy. They paid him late, while he himself had no new suit. With his wife, he had three children. Two daughters and a son. One of the girls, who had studied to be a lawyer, was killed in a car accident. Her sister lives with this painful wound. However, she is not one to feel sorry for herself. I have never met someone so accomplished! Though she hadn't had the chance to study, her intelligence evokes for me, that gift of intelligence that one asks of the Holy Spirit. She is also the friend in Cyprus with whom I can speak in Greek while being understood and while understanding what she is saying to me. If I don't know a word, she explains it to me in such a subtle and educational way. Her faith is a discreet accomplice, present in the smallest dish she prepares with benevolent hospitality. Omnipresent when it comes to praying for her loved ones or her friends, she also has a sense of beauty in all its forms. Always dressed with great taste and class. She is an outstanding cook, a mother, a balanced and balancing grandmother, an adorable wife. And a friend who became my Cypriot sister. The joy of living, of laughing, of chatting to excess! The joy of simply loving! Her husband reminds me of a lamb. Yet he is capable of yelling, to defend his opinions. But he has such a sweetness in his eyes that I sometimes think to myself, that it must have been easy to enslave a people with Christianity so deep rooted in its genes. Even if our guy is more likely to have coffee with his friends than go to church. Or go to the mountains in search of mushrooms and wild asparagus, a few portions of which he never fails to keep in the freezer for me. At 19 he married the woman of his life. She was 15, and they settled in Larnaca, while the family remained in the village. When in 1974 the Turks invaded this part of the island, the father was out working. The twelve-year-old, who had never driven, hurriedly loaded the family into the van. He hid them in the woods on an English base. Fortunately, it was August and the whole village took refuge there, waiting to build huts or be given tents. Their homes and possessions were looted, and some of those who ventured out at night to collect a few belongings never returned. As soon as our mushroom guy heard that his family was hiding in the woods, he rushed to bring everyone back to his home in Larnaca. Also, the expression "close-knit family" is not symbolic! He worked all his life in a large grocery store that was freezing in the winter and overheated in the summer. His wife, who worked in a not much more comfortable warehouse, told me that when she told him to buy a pair of new shoes, he replied: "Kids first, buy for the kids!" The kids were able to study. The beautiful girl is a teacher, while her brother left his calculations at the bank to become the priest we met on the road, that morning in July 1999. All his parishioners love him. Because he communicates to each of them the love of God, confidence and serenity. Obviously the trials of life spare no one, he faces them with courage and solidarity. Our friend's wife is a pharmacist. The very archetype of Greek beauty. Sparkling, always ready to share her joy. A mother as one dreams of having, juggling affection and the ability to rejoice in the unique path of each of her children. Yes I can affirm it, in Cyprus I met happy people!

14.

A NEW SEASON IN the OVEN

Once again July set Larnaca ablaze. I suffered and only felt relieved in the sea. My first agrypnia[60] on July 19th, 2001, feast of Saint Elie was an ordeal. Even though this church was vast with a high ceiling, I was literally suffocated there from seven in the evening until one in the morning. I wasn't even trying to spot Greek words that I knew anymore. I was trying to hold on! Because I felt that these rites, celebrated for centuries, were leading me towards a communion not only with those who were carnally present, but also

---

[60] Prayer vigil

with those who had prayed long before. In August, after the Agrypnia of the Feast of the Transfiguration, we were invited to the home of a couple, pillars of the parish, for a typical Cypriot evening soup. Despite my body's exhaustion, my heart was once again stuffed full with hospitality and kindness!

Our life gradually became that of the Cypriots. On Saturdays we went to the market which still extended over the whole main square. Bread, fruit and vegetables never exceeded 0.50 euros per kilo. We always went to the same trader. If a product wasn't good, he told us with a grimace not to buy it! One day when he was away, his wife explained to us that he was staying at the monastery for his holidays. In this district there were also many shops run by old people. Those who only the grave can stop. Shoemaker, carpenter, locksmith, dressmaker, tailor. They disappeared one after another. It was peaceful. It was alive. We felt at home. As for me, I felt better than at home. Of course the heatwave was a burden, especially for me. I tried to mitigate its harm by diving into the sea. That summer, I often travelled to the Metropol for my question-

and-answer sessions. I was hanging on! Is there any other way? And that is perhaps what strengthens us the most: the conquest. The hardships, the little demons, especially when they issue from our own bullshit! I learned the "Our Father" in Greek, which I still recite in that language, that shakes me up so much more deeply than my mother tongue, even if I am far from mastering it. After August 15th we decided to return to Troodos for a breather. No camping because of my crutches, but a modest boarding house in the forest, near the monastery of my love, the tiny monk. Before speaking of my mountain nook, I must go back to our first vespers service in the monks' chapel. It was October 1999. Wrapped in our red nylon jackets, ignorant of all "protocol", like not necessarily sitting right next to, let alone on top of, the monks. Or even kissing the hand of the gerondas, asking for his blessing. In short, two kangaroos disguised in red in a world blacker than black! I had understood absolutely nothing other than my usual three words and sincerely I did not keep a poignant memory of it. Except for the rustle of our nylon jackets every time we got up, sat down again or even made our signs of the cross. Yet we went back! I am tempted, without any pretensions, to add that we were "pushed" to go back! Once again, hold tight and don't let go!

"Maria, what are you looking for?"

In this second half of August 2001, I still had no answer...

15.

IN THE NOOK OF THE MOUNTAIN, IN THE NOOK OF MY LOVE

We went to the monastery in the early afternoon. After our picnic under the pines a few hundred metres from the entrance. This is where, one day, we met a dishevelled monk who was picking herbs as wild as he was. I dusted off my best Greek to ask him when it was time for vespers. "4:30 p.m." Not another word, before continuing on his way. With the cunning of the fox in The Little Prince[61], I ended up taming him during my repeated stays. I have lost count of the afternoons spent chatting with him, while he cracked nuts, sorted apples or roamed the garden. As for the harvested plants, a few years later we always left with a big bag of sage for the winter. Over time, I managed not only to make myself understood, but to understand what was being said to me. A moving story about this illiterate child who was now 80 years old. "It was the monks who taught me to read and write!" His candid faith is a lesson. One day while he was sweeping the yard, he said to me, "And those who were not born Orthodox like me? How could it possibly be that there is no place in heaven for them?" His experimental theology ran aground on God's love. Also, his dusty cap hid beneath it a look of poignant kindness. His grandfather lived in a house where the walls and floor were made of earth. He always laughed during this story: "Fortunately, because the family buried what they owned, when the pirates came, only the big table was there!" He also told

---

[61] In Saint-Exupéry's *The Little Prince*, the fox tells the little prince to sit a bit closer to him every day.

me that his brother, engaged in EOKA, committed attacks at night. While he, holed up in his room, shuddered as soon as he heard an explosion. "Me, I was a quiet child!" I also know that it was he who went to the bus stop, along with my love, the tiny monk, to welcome the young neophyte who had left everything to enter the monastery.

This man, he was an engineer graduate who had studied in England. With such a background, all he had to do was embark on a great career. Yet his heart also came to a stop, in the nook of the mountain. All that remained was to get his parents, who had made so many sacrifices for his studies, to swallow the bitter pill. One night on the terrace, the silence seemed conducive to revelations. He then launched into his news: "I want to become a monk." The silence engulfed itself in an endless silence, protected by this knowing night. Not a reproach, not a question, not a word, not a sound. So he worked to repay his parents for their expenses, then he set off on the mountain road trembling a little. When my love the tiny monk and my dishevelled monk greeted him, his doubts vanished. Having become a theologian and hieromonk[62], he is not only a precious help to the gerondas but also a witness, even on social networks, with his unconditional love for the Orthodox tradition. The hours I spent in his office were a collection of pearls that, if they haven't made me a better person, have the merit of reminding me of the grime in my soul. It was one of the Cypriot encounters that grafted me to that benevolent insistence on the heart's prayer[63] that he calls our breathing.

And then there is the gardener who flutters about in the huge, terraced garden. With the same ease, he slips into the chapel for the services. As if all was only angelic lightness. I don't know anything about him. On the other hand, he asked non-stop questions. About our church, the language in which Pierre celebrated, about the singers, the faithful. Or the climate at home, the animals in the forests, the fruits and vegetables that grow there. He also introduced me to the secrets of their garden. With him I learned about the ecology of yesteryear in these poor regions. I

---

[62] Priest monk
[63] Lord Jesus Christ, Son of God, have mercy on me!

learned to recognise wild goat tracks. I learned how to get rid of mosquitoes without insecticides. By digging a pond of stagnant water with large fish that eat their eggs and larvae. I was filled up with seasonal fruits, as I have never eaten elsewhere. What I am about to say will sound silly, but with him, as with the other monks, I understood why Saint Paul writes that in Christ: "...There is no longer...either man or woman..."[64] Because I have never felt so free and so pure in my relationships. One day he asked me like a curious child, to bring him pictures of the city where we lived. The postcards we shared during our next stay, showing the four seasons, delighted him so much, that he wanted loads of details. That day I said to myself that yes, heavenly sweetness existed, and that I had shared it in the nook of the mountain, in the nook of my love.

Gentleness is still what defines the hieromonk who often took the services, worked in the bookshop or even baked bread every Tuesday. After studying theology in Athens, he became a

---

[64] Galatians 3:26-29

monk. Another of those faces that you see in fairy tales. Whether he talks to me about theology or lets me discover the secrets of how his bread is made, again with ancestral methods, such as sorting the flour on a sieve to remove the worms, the tone of his voice remains unchanged. We get tired of monotony, we don't get tired of a voice chiselled by prayer. My most precious gift was to leave with a little prosphora[65] that he had made. For me it was a work of art. With him, I learned to listen to the whispering of angels, in the nook of the mountain, in the nook of my love.

Dietary restrictions due to my health concerns were quickly registered. It should be noted that the picnics had been replaced by meals at the monastery in a small room, close to the cell made available to us. After meals, I went to the kitchen to thank the cook and chat with him. A cook by trade, he had worked in a large hotel in Rhodes. We talked about religion, cooking recipes and monastic gossip. He made me a herbal tea, and I watched him with his huge saucepans, assisted by a monk whose background was unusual to say

---

[65] Bread that will be consecrated for the Holy Communion.

the least. Of German origin, he had worked as a train driver. One day on holiday, he found himself in the nook of the mountain. Love at first sight, since he gave up everything to enter the monastery. When his mother became weak, and there was no place in a home, he left to take care of her. I wondered if I would see him again. He came back! How can we forget this fraternity under the protection of the Mother of God? This still-intact nature too. This calm of the night with the scent of wild roses. I remember the first night spent at the monastery with the crossing of the courtyard, accompanied by a monk and his torch. Absolute silence. It was around 3 a.m. and we were alone in the world, surrounded by these unforgettable smells. And especially the Church of the Mother of God with the offices of prayers which, although they make the body sore, strengthen the soul in its conquest. How I understand that our train driver could not do without it! But do not fantasize, all this comes with a price. That of an immense asceticism for years. A whole life, in the purest monastic tradition. With schedules that leave little time for the heart to frolic. In the nook of the night, in the nook of my mountain, the monks, awakened at 03:00, begin their hearts' prayer, before meeting in the church for the services and the liturgy. Around 7:30 a.m. a snack followed by a personal reading, with a thought that will occupy the monk during his diakonia. Chores with the buildings or in the garden, which must support spiritual life. 10.30 a.m. a new office before the 11.30 a.m. meal. Two hours of rest and work resumes until Vespers at 4:30 p.m. Dinner, then the evening office after which the monks meet for a teaching. For decades, this took place around the hegumen, the backbone of the current monastery, as I have known it. In this year 2022, 82 years of monastic life and 52 years as hegumen.

What fate! At the age of three, he was struck down by an illness that nearly killed him. Death before death, for this colossus who likes to recall the phrase of Saint Neophytos: "The most precious good above all goods is the fear of God and the memory of death." As a child, he loved to sleep crouched at his mother's feet. When she died, the six-year-old boy was told that from now on his mother would be the Virgin Mary. His father, a cantor at the village church, initiated him into the mysteries of the song of angels, and his attraction to the life of prayer was revealed at an early age. He was twelve years old when a new ordeal struck him. During the freezing winter, his father also died. Heartbroken, he once again turned to the sky. Towards the Eternal Father. To help the family survive, he worked in the asbestos mines. However, the young man refused to work on Sunday, which was consecrated to God. One day, his annoyed brother shouted at him: "Go to the monastery!" He obeyed him to the letter and packed his bundle. There he was at 17, landing in the nook of my mountain. The buildings were in poor condition, the living conditions spartan and the climate very harsh. The hegumen at that time said to him by way of welcome: "If you manage to make it through the winter, then you can stay!" To stay, thanks to the protection of the Mother of God! 82 years ago! Elected hegumen in his turn, he travelled through the monasteries, especially those of the Holy Mountain[66], in search of a rule suited to his

---

[66] Ibid. 8

community. As for the buildings, they were gradually restored. An iconographer himself, inviting heaven to descend to earth, he participated in the restoration work. I have never come across a more successful marriage between rightness and mercy. To put right what is twisted with the constant concern of God's love. Around the world, this attitude often turns into a fiasco that is described in French as "milk soup", or a boiling over. I believe the secret lies in surrendering one's own will to the will of God. Then what you do is never the reaction of a wounded ego or inconvenient confusion. It's inscribed in the purification of the rectified person's heart. Yes, in the nook of the mountain, in the nook of my love, I felt the fruitful mystery of the Akrivia-Ekonomia[67] antinomy, the theory that gets taught in the institutes of theology.

The first time we were invited to his office, so as to introduce him to the two kangaroos who were bent on returning to his monastery, I was very impressed. I only came out with a few banalities, when nothing was asked of me! As for

---

[67] Justice, rightness and restraint, mercy.

the colossus, he seemed to save his words. I understood later that he never wasted them, reserving his energy for prayer. Over the years I ended up relaxing, during the unforgettable herbal tea sessions on the bench where he used to sit. It was there that he told me that death was a gift from God, when I came to seek comfort after my dad's passing, then my brother's. It may shock. This shocked me! But I realised that the whole life of the monks, their fasting, their asceticism, their prayer had only one goal, that of achieving union with God. And of course to be prepared for this union at the time of death. There were also lighter herbal teas, and I had the grace to discover on that ascetic face the most angelic smile of light. When we thanked him for his hospitality, he replied: "One day I will offer you hospitality in paradise!" Once again, I have never come across a more perfect alliance between maturity, experience and candid naivety.

One evening at vespers I went, as always, to kiss his hand before the service. A perceptible warmth emanated from it that I can neither describe nor decipher. For a few seconds I was enveloped in a universe beyond any rational explanation, immersed in that of Love purified by decades of asceticism and prayers. Yes, in the nook of my mountain, in the nook of my love, I encountered an authentic pure heart!

Modern psychologists will speak of an orphaned child's incredible resilience who, moreover, came close to death at the age of three. A resilience that has borne countless fruits, starting with his intact soul on the eve of his hundredth birthday. Fruit, not only for his monks, but also for other "children" he took care of. Not to mention a nun's monastery, a home for the elderly and a crèche. Since adolescence I have met a plethora of spiritual people of all stripes, healers and therapists. But this "path of resilience" which has no other purpose than that of union with God, placed me for the very first time before a pneumatic colossus, imbued carnally with the divine presence!

It is undoubtedly this quest for the kingdom of heaven, which he defines as the sole goal of monastic life, which engraved this true humility in him. When in 2010 the Holy Synod of Cyprus came to honour him, he returned the honour to the four monks with whom he had started his journey in the nook of the mountain. In recounting their lives and their last moments, he called them holy fathers. Ending his homage with The One who made going through so many trials possible, The Mother of God.

When his health deteriorated, he increasingly went away to a less harsh climate, where he could receive appropriate care. Every time I entered the offices and saw his empty chair, I felt a kind of unease. As if the monks and I with them were orphans. Yes, in the nook of my mountain, in the nook of my love, I felt that one could love someone like an unrelated father.

It is to express this affection to him that in 20 18, led by a friend who was staying in the neighbourhood, I went to visit him in his place of retirement. He replied that we were in the same Corps[68], which made the bonds so strong. His moving candour was intact. He smiled: "Today I will write in my diary that presbyterate Maria of France, travelled all the way to visit me!" He added with the look of an exile that if I

---

[68] The body of Christ.

had come with my car, we would both have gone back to the monastery. He also missed the nook of the mountain. I confided to him "that I had no courage for asceticism and combat…that I was afraid of illness. Of suffering. Of old age. Of death…"[69] And I asked him to bless me. Kneeling in front of the colossus, whose infirmity had in no way diminished the intensity of his Presence, I waited for him to "place his two long, very long, old hands on my head"[70]. Spark of eternity. The one that embraces peace. The crowning moment of those twenty years of chosen, wished-for, conquering returns. When he accompanied me back to the door with his walker, he proudly showed me that he had installed a bicycle bell and a lamp. He stopped right in front of the door, raising his hand in farewell. As a sign of A Dieu, having just advised me not to forget this prayer: "My God, keep me close to you always!"

He is always assisted by the monastery nurse who follows him everywhere, and whose absence is also felt in the community. Another unique

---

[69] *Sparkles of Intensity,* Maria Andreas (Huge Jam 2020)
[70] Ibid. 69

face, a hypostasis as we say in theological language. Each hypostasis being distinct while remaining united to the others. For him, it is about proclaiming God's love to all winds, jubilant when this wind brings back conversions. Strangers who were just passing through. Sometimes he joked, "I'm jealous, because you're going swimming! When I was a child, I walked for miles to go swimming." And then he had his favourite trick that he told us one morning when he left the office: "I have a secret to tell you." He then whispered in French: "I love you!" During one of my many walks in the garden, I met him and he said to me: "Maria, you are with us in our offices, you are dressed in black like us, ask the gerondas to stay with us!" In the evening near my big oak tree, looking at this garden that I loved so much, I wondered if I would have had the courage. My too-damaged carcass did not even allow me the dream of an answer. I also remembered the day when, after the complete monastic cycle, I had to leave in a hurry. Caught up by one of my famous digestive discomforts. Pierre had then realistically concluded: "You could not begin such an ascetic life now!" That's right, and I'm grateful for my unique life, too. However, it is in the nook of the mountain, in the nook of my love that I left forever, the best part of my heart...

Over time, in my dear monastery, I began to experience the impactful richness of the Greek language. This time from ancient Greek, preserved in the offices. I was lucky to be able to benefit from the help of my confessor with the beautiful white beard. He explained to me what was sometimes impossible to translate. The services which at the beginning had seemed endless to me, slowly became impregnated in me. Thanks to my reading and practice in French at home, I was able to find my bearings better. But in fact, from the start, I renounced both the process of translation and that of intellectual understanding. And what happened surprisingly is that I was sometimes caught by a word or an expression that dragged me into a theological shock of the heart. And this with phrases that I had been repeating for more than thirty years, without any effect. Among these shocks, there is one that particularly marked me. It was in February, in the middle of Lent. Pierre accompanied me and we took the road to my mountain. There was snow and even fallen boulders. A thick fog not only meant that we did not pass anyone, but I clung to the steering wheel praying, as the hieromonk had taught me. The latter, however, had expressed his surprise that we had come this far. At the chapel service surrounded by fog, with the monks and their long black Lenten veils, signs of penitance[71], I felt on another planet. And I was! At the end of the service, the 14 monks in front of the iconostasis all sang the Lenten song together: "Kyrie ton Dinameon..." with vigour. It was for me a new perception of God, felt for the duration of the hymn. Attached to the sweetness of God, that day in the nook of the mountain, in the nook of my love, I met the Almighty God!

Returning in September 2001 descending into the furnace, I still didn't know exactly what I was looking for, but I had a certainty. As long as I can get back to my mountain, I'll be back!

---

[71] The Greek word, metanoia, isn't anything to do with guilt-inducing flagellation but means above all giving a new direction to your heart so that, little by little, the inflated ego is replaced by the Other.

16.

MY LITTLE PORT

The bathing resumed, my body finding more and more solace in the Cypriot sea. Gradually we became familiar with the small fishing port we passed through every day. Another world that had to be tamed. Once again language was key. Even though my first friend spoke gibberish, a mixture of Cypriot, English and whatever else he could fit. He was the adventurer, the atypical of the port. He was not a professional fisherman, but had worked as a policeman. A former resistance fighter, he had lost an eye in battle, the secrets of which I have never been able to penetrate. If I had to compare him to an animal,

I would choose one of those wild cats that always lands on its feet. I remember a gift that could only have come from him. Although late into the profession, having brought back a magnificent boat from Syria, he was a shrewd fisherman. He told me in advance which shoals of fish would pass near the coast. That year, the day before we left, it was the turn of the tuna. Proud of his catch, he had wrapped two huge slices of fresh tuna for us in newspaper. A little surprised that we didn't slip this bloody present into our suitcase! One day he met a Chinese woman with whom he fell madly in love. This is how he lost control of his life. After many adventures and round trips to Beijing, he ended up marrying her and following her to her country. He found himself ruined a few years later, after fleeing Beijing, where he had built a house for his beloved. Ill, he had been given treatment in a dodgy hospital, where they had not even changed the sheets when he entered. On his return he sold his boat and disappeared from the port. But it was misunderstanding this soldier to think that he would abdicate! One day while I was chatting with friends on the pavement, a car stopped. My radiant adventurer came out shouting: "I recognised your voice Maria!" Reunions, embraces and biography. He had just met a Chinese woman, "an adorable, very small one who would take care of him in his old age..."

His neighbour at the port had a large completely uncovered boat. Whatever the season, he never wore a hat and had a scorched face, highlighted by very expressive eyes. All the more expressive as he was deaf and mute. He emitted a few cries-groans but these were absolutely incomprehensible. Every evening he went to cast his nets and at dawn he would gather them. Beaming when the fishing was good, beaming when it wasn't. Looking up at the sky, he indicated by signs what the next day would bring. We became friends, and I quickly learned to read his lips. We spent countless evenings in port "running on", as we like to do so much in Cyprus. The ritual had become a routine. When I was taking my evening walk and he arrived, I would catch the rope thrown onto the quay. As soon as the boat was moored, we sat on the small wall opposite. He was so funny, even with dramatic subjects. He had a way of miming them that made them comical. Transparent and without hypocrisy. It is certain that I laughed more with him than with soporific well-spoken and well-meaning people!

On the other side of my adventurer's boat, there was a small, frail and shy man. Widowed for a long time, he contented himself with bringing back just enough to eat. Often it was a big octopus that he would drag around always in the same old plastic bag. We ended up exchanging a few words, but I never knew his life. His dilapidated house was on my way when I went to Saint Lazare, and I sometimes saw him wandering around. It must be said that at that time, Cyprus and especially this old district of Larnaca, was still inhabited by modest people who had complete confidence in their neighbours. As a result, the doors of their homes were wide open day and night. One evening, more talkative than usual, he told me that he had remarried the very young Pakistani woman who ran his household. Shortly after, he died of a heart attack...

However, there were also happy and balanced fathers among my friends. Like the one with the loudest voice in the port. A voice impossible to miss, even from a thousand leagues under the sea! An excellent fisherman, we enjoyed his fish for years. He spoke in the most faithful Cypriot dialect, which amounts to saying that you have to forget your Greek, to embark on pure intuition! I think I have a bit of that gift, so we ended up talking too. A refugee from Famagusta[72], he liked to evoke the crystal clear and fish-filled coasts of his hometown. His dear city, since the invasion of 1974, has become a ghost town. His sober and peaceful wife often undid the nets with him. He worked hard and paid for the education of his two sons, the eldest of whom found a good job in a bank. The youngest has opened a small bistro which is doing well. Neither took over the boat, even though the father explained that the most beautiful moments of his life began at three in the morning. When the beauty was purring outside the port, and he found himself between sky and sea with the murmur of the waves. Every time I returned to my island and arrived at the

---

[72] In the north of the island, occupied by the Turkish republic since the 1974 Turkish invasion.

port, I heard the thunder calling me: "*Kalos orises, Maria!*"[73] He underwent two operations to his spine, and we swapped clinical experiences. Others to his heart which contributed to that one day, the only one where I found him with a sad face, when he murmured: "It's over, I can no longer go to sea!" Pained in my turn, I found only one stupid question as consolation: "And the boat?" It should be noted that it was a jewel of a boat, polished after each return to sea and repainted many times. He replied with a mocking smile and tears in his eyes: "It'll do for tourists, we'll place it on the roundabout at the entrance to my village!" This happened to be the roundabout that leads to my Cypriot parish, so every Sunday I passed the gleaming boat once again. But he was too attached to the port, to his quarrels, to his laughter with friends, so every day he comes in his van to sell vegetables, fruit or snails. He then sits down with his coffee at the cabin that serves as the captaincy and engages in heated debates. He has aged too, but I was relieved to find him one evening in October

---

[73] Welcome Maria!

2021, when I started this story.

The last on the list is still a successful family man. His wife sometimes comes to get the fish for the restaurants. His boat is by far the most modern and imposing. Always impeccable, it slides every morning to find the friends who will come to undo the nets, and the buyers, including myself. I have always been treated to Cypriot fare from this gorgeous man, dressed all in black. Eyes as black as his clothes. Displaying a contrast with the white of his hair and his artfully trimmed beard. Even less than the Cypriot rate, after he found out that Pierre was a priest. He often answered me, when I asked him the price of my bag of fish: "I want the father's blessing!" I don't think I'll meet many fishermen anymore who will tell me that. Because the younger generation only cares about profitability. Going so far as to despise that custom of naming a boat after a saint, so that it might be blessed and placed under the protection of prayer. In the age of radars and smartphones, it is more and more becoming a memory that the sea, I am sure, will never forget! If I have one piece of advice to give to the new wave that is, in its turn, going into the waves, it is to not throw overboard that tradition that forged the soul of its ancestors. That treasure that anchored in my little port that unique link, which still connects the sea, the sky and the earth!

17.

NEW CYPRIOT AUTUMN

After the summer break, Greek classes resumed in September at Larnaca High School. We became friends with the headteacher who invited us to his son's wedding, and with the biology teacher. A priest[74], doctor of biology. Another of those beings who flit through life with angelic lightness! An innate kindness, a brilliant intelligence and a concern for his parishioners down to the smallest details of their lives. But above all, that sublime marriage of science and

---

[74] Orthodox priests are married and have families and jobs, if they are not monks.

theology! What better way to dream of blocking the way to obscurantism or to that omnipresent temptation to slip into monophysitism[75]. Life did not spare him. An orphan, a refugee too, he had been brought up by his godfather. A remarkable man whom we met during a sumptuous Easter meal. His wife, with her feet firmly on the ground, held the house with energy, tenderness and humour. Their four children have had a brilliant career abroad. The liturgies at his parish were impressive, as he celebrated like a dancer on a rope. After my multiple health journeys, cancer, which he learned about, we lost sight of each other. Recently, I wanted to come back to his church. At the end of the liturgy, I came forward last to greet him. His wife, who recognised me immediately, accompanied me. He stopped, hesitated. So she said to him: "But it's Maria!"

---

[75] Heretical doctrine asserting that Christ has only a divine nature which has absorbed human nature. It sounds gibberish, but this heresy excludes human synergy. To trivialise slightly, we could say for example that science is useless, since God does everything! Whereas the theology of the councils, according to which Christ is God AND Man, opens the door to divine-human collaboration in all its forms.

He probably didn't expect to see me again, because he burst into tears as he hugged me. Yes, in Cyprus, we still know how to cry with emotion and tenderness, and as a bonus, it's done in front of a superb iconostasis!

Our return was planned for the end of October. One day Pierre had the intuition to go to the shipping agency to check the dates. This allowed us to return with the car, because we learned that the very last Limassol-Piraeus journey with cars in the hold would take place on October 23rd. It was therefore necessary to leave the big rock a week in advance, which did not please me. Knowing that we could no longer drive back, we left two large suitcases with a friend.

We had begun to listen regularly to this radio to which I owe so many services, homilies and music. Radio Kiti, the very one that caught my heart on our first trip. The main announcer with such a soothing voice announces everything that is important in the church. Thus we learned that on October 18th in Aradipou[76], the parish of

---

[76] Suburb of Larnaca

Saint Luc would welcome not only the relics of the doctor-evangelist, but also the child of the country, the hegumen Ephraim of Vatopedi. This will amuse atheists, and once again I understand it. We welcome relics as we would a living being. In Cyprus the tradition is still preserved, and it is an event when a saint is received in a procession. With the participation of the clergy, the faithful but also politicians, the police, the brass band and schools. We arrived that evening to a packed church. My crutches gave me priority to one of those seats thanks to which the back is supported even while standing. Thirsty after the long offices, we entered a huge tent. Hegumen Ephraim was chatting at the counter, his back turned. I approached slowly. Suddenly he turned around and blessed me, before I had time to ask. I have often thought of that sudden turn and that blessing, which with hindsight I feel to be a kind of viaticum[77], for the trials that were hanging over me!

---

[77] Eucharist for someone close to, or in danger of, death.

18.

THE TRIALS

I will not dwell on this subject, described in my book: *Illness, My Complicit Enemy*.[78] We resumed our Greek lessons at the university with the idea, at least for me, of leaving as soon as possible! Especially since I had made my decision to reconnect with a canonical Orthodox Church. A few days before being received at the parish of Saint Joseph in Bordeaux, I had my usual mammogram. A dozen more followed. Not hard to guess why! Just two very aggressive differentiated breast tumours. Here I am

---

[78] Maria Andreas (Amazon 2018) preface by Professor Gérard Ostermann, Bordeaux

embarked on the fight that many women have gone through before me. I took the icon of the Virgin and after each waking up from anaesthetic I contemplated her saying to Pierre: "You will take me back there!" I was encouraged to do so by the professor who operated on me. Especially with the hope of curing through swimming my frozen shoulder after the axillary lymphadenectomy. So we had a short stay there just after the radiotherapy. Time to realise how the sea would now be my best ally. We took the opportunity to drop by my patron saint. I received the grace of wearing her miraculous belt that is in the monastery. What an emotion to find my big oak! To hear a familiar monk explain to another I didn't know: "It's Maria, she had a serious operation!" He had not only prayed for me, he had not forgotten. Because in the nook of my mountain, in the nook of my love, we have the memory of the heart. The one who hangs on when the other falters!

Moving forward on two crutches with a "torn" shoulder had become an ordeal. Also the decision to have a hip replacement was made for mid-December. If all went well, that was one year too many. I sank into both somatic and psychological exhaustion. But I had a light in that winter night of 2002-2003. Find the nook of my mountain, the nook of my love! So I performed my hip and shoulder physio sessions relentlessly.

April 2003 I was walking without crutches with the recommendation to go swimming for my shoulder. Even though the physiotherapist later told me that she'd judged that it was irrecoverable, a year of swimming overcame the mobility problem. So here I am patched up for more than ever, to return to my island!

19.

A PASSAGE THROUGH NAFKAPTOS[79]

Here I'm opening a parenthesis to talk about Pierre's progress in the Greek language, and a "fortuitous" discovery that was to prove a turning point in our lives. It was the summer of 2001. In the heat of the furnace, Pierre left in the morning to work at the air-conditioned library in Larnaca. While he had been waiting for years for a connection between psychology and theology, the very first book he pulled off the shelves seemed to be what he had been looking

---

[79] Small port in the Corinthian Gulf

for for a long time: *Orthodox Psychotherapy* by Metropolitan Hierotheos Vlachos[80]. What a happy "chance", because during the year that we spent at the diakonia of Zürich near my hospitals, he translated this seminal work. Armed with large dictionaries and a desire to deepen this tradition of purification of the heart. His tenacity enabled us to meet the author of the book in 2004, this great theologian, ascetic, anchored deeply in Jesus's prayer, the Metropolitan Hierotheos, with whom we had the good fortune to become friends. As well as with the nuns of the Greek monastery of Lebadeia who publish all his works. Among them Catechesis and the Baptism of adults, another gem that Pierre has translated. We would need a new book to tell of our travels in Greece, but I will content myself with the first in April 2004 from Larnaca. Once again we looked like two lost kangaroos, even if we had shortened our red jackets into more ecclesial outfits. The intensity of the encounter, benevolent hospitality and above all hospitality from the heart! Though proud of my new hip, I

---

[80] French translation: Pierre Deschamps

experienced that obscuring veil that falls across the senses, ready to smother them. We were contaminated, no doubt from water or cheese that was not fresh. As I was the most fragile, I had my dose! So we left earlier than expected. I see myself on the plane to Larnaca with my litre of coke. Slipping into a taxi on arrival, to start an endless spate of vomiting. I didn't think you could vomit so much. Or have so much headache. After a few hours I started to zone out, and Pierre called an ambulance. I remember the name of one of the paramedics, Séraphin, who was trying to find out what I had eaten or drunk. When I left the hospital, after a week of rest, I almost came back to life the day I was able to dive into my dear ally! For the record, this did not prevent us from returning several times to Greece, in particular to Nafpaktos. Each return being a precious episode of life, an unforgettable gift, for which I would like to thank God, our dearest Metropolitan Hierotheos and all the wonderful friends of Nafpaktos.

20.

THE TWO CYPRIOT FAMILIES ARE GROWING

The family "from above" has continued to grow. Local saints like Saint Epiphanius[81] or Saint Neophytos, but also those whose relics were passing through. I planned my flights so as not to miss the feast of Sainte Thecla or Saint George. But Saint Lazarus remains my favourite. I arrived at the beginning of the week of services marking his death to his resurrection[82], with the procession through the streets of Larnaca of

---

[81] Great saint and Cypriot theologian. Feast day 12th May, my birthday!
[82] Saturday evening, Palm Sunday Eve

which he is the patron saint. When my body no longer allowed me to stay for hours in a crowded church, I went there in the evening for vespers or simply during the day. It is impossible to describe these experiences which ultimately remain very personal. Even if the prayer of the faithful around their bishop already captures the energies of Life. The smells of incense, perfume, flowers. But above all the relationship with the one we come to kiss, simply because he has become a close friend.

The family "from below" has also welcomed new members. The first we had already met in 1999, when we filled up with gas at his garage. A tall, sympathetic fellow with broad shoulders and a tanned face. He told us that he had been a captain of a merchant ship. Little by little we discovered that we had the same parish, and that he too had planned a stay at the Holy Mountain. Emerging from this man was a rare quiet strength. His principles are old-fashioned like ours, like putting his family at the centre of his life, his work without ever complaining, whether it's 45 degrees or an icy wind. I discovered over the years that this square old boy was the most loyal, the most available and the most generous of all my friends. And this with modest discretion. It is thanks to him and his younger brother that I was able to keep driving, independent for more than twenty years. One evening we all went to the fish restaurant. This is where we met his wife. As small as her husband is tall, always delighted with a good meal and a glass of wine. Never in 20 years have I heard her say that something was wrong, even though her life also had its share of hardship. She glides over the years with that face of serenity that we immediately notice in her eyes. One evening in childhood, the night light by the Mother of God icon had run out of oil. She heard the Virgin call her by her first name, saying to her: "I want some oil!" In her home, ever since, there has been a lit tealight in front of the Virgin. A night light also shining permanently in her eyes. Our captain must have cracked immediately on seeing those two jewels. When they first met, he asked her out for coffee. And it was in front of this cup of coffee that he asked her: "Shall we get married? Instant response: "Okay, let's marry!" That was 40 years ago. Since then, two splendid boys have been born, and they have settled by the sea that our sailor cannot help but contemplate. I remember certain principles imposed on his adolescents that touched me. One Sunday after the liturgy, we had a hearty breakfast facing the sea. One of the boys came to ask his father for the key to the car. "Okay, but first you visit your grandmother!" Happy grandmother, in this case his mother-in-law, whom I had the chance to know. Jovial, greedy, hospitable. Yet they lost everything too! Lost everything during the Turkish invasion of 1974, and they are still exiles! When the borders were opened, they went to see their house again. Only ruins remained, even the table legs had been sawn off. When I started this story, I found myself on the veranda of the house by the sea, enjoying not only a meal put together by our captain, but also this transparent sharing, so authentic. Yes in Cyprus, hearts are still capable of a faithful and deep friendship!

I was not the only one to enjoy their hospitality. Our captain's wife welcomed a "lost" Englishwoman into her heart. After a journey worthy of a Charles Dickens novel, this torn woman came to pick up the pieces of her life in Cyprus. She was accompanied by a benevolent husband, resolutely British! She, on the other hand, integrated into our parish. After having followed a long catechesis with my Cypriot confessor, she was baptised Orthodox. And she ended up persuading her husband to marry her in church. In this same church where she was buried. I attended the funeral of this pure Briton, originally from the former coloniser! She passed on Resurrection Sunday! What a beautiful symbol for one of the most sublime mysteries of Life, that of Reconciliation in all its forms! I hasten to add that the links between England and Cyprus are very fruitful. Many English retirees come to seek the sun all year round, especially near Paphos. As for the Cypriots, they have a large community in England. Every family I know has at least one member studying or working there. Often settled, they marry and start a family in what has become their second homeland.

The youngest of the family below is not Cypriot, but Russian. The presence of foreign women is sometimes viewed with suspicion.

Because some, looking like models, did not hesitate to hook the first gullible voyeur, eager for those superb bodies that were being shown off with the arrogance that beauty gives! My "big kid" entered into a love marriage with a divorced Cypriot friend. In 2013, Cyprus, where one of the main banks went bankrupt, went through a crushing economic crisis. Some lost their life savings, others their jobs, and my "big kid's" family was not spared. No more work for the father who admitted to me one day: "While many wives would have left, mine stayed united!" Unflinchingly taking care of the building with patience and humility. As always, beware of generalities and hasty judgments! I cannot help adding in this month of April 2022 that not all Russians are executioners or billionaire oligarchs. I met many of them in Cyprus, and I would like to tell them how I remember their sincere aspiration for a peaceful life! Other sufferings did not fail to upset my "big kid", but she always showed courage and resilience. Intelligent, cultured, speaking perfect Greek, she educates her three children so that they might hold on to their freedom, thanks to their studies. Each of these teas spent sharing "miraculous" virtues, was a slap in the face to the trials that have peppered our lives, in addition to being a hymn to friendship! And speaking of friendship, on either the ground or higher storey, her best friend since I have known her, is a Ukrainian...

21.

DRAMA ON MOUNT ATHOS, MOURNING IN CYPRUS

It was September 2004. Cyprus Airways only departed from Amsterdam. Arriving there from Zürich, we boarded the blue and white airbus with its symbol of the Troodos sheep. Before us sat four Greek nuns. Pierre told them he was an Orthodox priest. So they asked us if we were also going to Cyprus for the funeral. This is how we learned of the drama at Mount Athos. Patriarch Petros of Alexandria, himself originally from Cyprus, had been flying in a helicopter that crashed into the Aegean Sea, shortly before it was due to arrive at The Holy Mountain. Sixteen passengers had perished with him, including the hegumen Arsenios of the monastery of Machairas. We had met his beautiful and so youthful smile during services in Machairas, and when he had consecrated a nun in a new monastery. Child of Larnaca, the hegumen Arsenios was mourned not only by his family, but by the whole city. It was with emotion that we saw our two priest friends carry the large coffin into the monastery cemetery. Yes, in Cyprus, the incomprehensible also manages to strike, and despite the hope of the Resurrection, crushes hearts.

22.

THE FAT PIG

As I said before, not all men go to church. Or for those who don't attend, not all of them have that reflex of a married friend who only attends services other than weddings, funerals and baptisms: "When I meet a superb girl that I want, I stop at the next church. I light a candle there and entrust my thoughts to God!" Innate reaction, of a people who for generations have practiced confession, which current doctors are beginning to recognise as a liberating act. Alas, I'm not sure that the one I ended up calling "the fat pig" belongs to this trend. He wasn't the only one circling the beach district, inviting females to get into his car. But he was violent and scared me. He even happened to jump on a tourist in the sea. So much so that seeing him, I went swimming elsewhere. A crazy libido, at the limit of what's bearable. Extremely strong, his face burned and his eyes emptied by his passion. One day I remembered that you should love your enemies. Yes, yes, he had become my enemy, since he had come out of his car furious after my rejection, and I had taken refuge with a couple of passers-by. Failing in my efforts to love him, I began to pray for "the big pig from the beach"! This calmed me down, which will seem obvious, even to an atheist. I also realised that my too transparent blouse could, despite my age, attract obsessed looks. Since then I adapted my outfit perfectly. A thick man's shirt, large misshapen trousers, that make his Mercedes go on its way. This is called the chameleon technique! I wanted to pray, but not expose myself to the martyrdom of a sex maniac! One day, I no longer saw him. I was pretentious enough to imagine that my prayers had taken him away from his vice! One afternoon I was chatting with two friends who run a bookstore. Then I saw my big pig arrive.

Bent over, panting, advancing like a centenarian. I admit to a moment of secret satisfaction, thinking that he would do no more harm. He then begins to tell us that he almost died, and that his heart had undergone a major operation. I found myself asking God to bless him as he jolted out. An involuntary prayer, but it too, O how much a generator of peace! If there is a benefit to be derived from services and pilgrimages, it is this kind of reflex that arises instead of revenge or another feeling with destructive energies. I go further, I believe that words, sacred gestures are so many electrons of life. Besides, I imagine that my big pig did not escape it, because before painfully leaving our bookstore, he murmured: "*Doxa To Theo!*"[83], the open sesame of Orthodoxy! Neither he nor I left the store with an exemplary soul. Worse, his obsessive passion did not remain within hospital walls. I met him recently at the beach. He was waving, clumsily because of his weakened heart, at female tourists. I couldn't help thinking of this saying whose translation does not resonate as

---

[83] Glory to God!

well as in Greek, where we play on the sonorous rhyme of the two words flesh and tombstone. The meaning is this: "The fight of the flesh ends under the tombstone!"

While hunters of females are frequent and for the most part harmless, not all single men are obsessed with the first bikini. Many have become friends with whom I willingly exchanged a few words before swimming. There is one I would like to tell a moving anecdote about. It was 1999. There was only one rock I could squeeze through with my back. However, it was sometimes already occupied by a bundle of bones roasting in the sun. One day I told this skeleton that it was the only rock where I could put my things. Since then, as soon as I arrived, he got up and stuck his long body between two less welcoming rocks. I found this gesture gallant and I asked him his first name. Soft and shy smile accompanied his response. The next day I brought him a small icon of the Virgin Mary. Shortly after, his scooter was stolen. Sweet, shy smile in protest. My skeletal neighbour was definitely not the violent type. So I never saw him again. During my most recent stay, having opted for the nearest large beach of Larnaca, I saw my still-emaciated skeleton on a rock by the sea. It had been over 20 years! I called over to him, but he had trouble recognising me, which I understand! Then he laughed and we chatted a bit. We talked about his village, but he was unable to tell me who its patron saint was. I concluded that the skeleton with the soft and shy smile was more at the café than at the church. By the way, this was confirmed when he brought me gossip from his coffee buddies about Covid. The next day he came up to me proud, like a kid who had just pulled off a prank. Guess what he was holding in his hand? The icon of the Mother of God that I gave him 23 years ago! Yes, even for a fervent devotee of the village café, unaware of the saint who is protecting it, in Cyprus The Most Holy Mother of God is sacred and we take care of her!

23.

THE CYPRIOT FAMILY IS STILL GROWING

I wanted to write "family from below", but if these nuns are from below, their hearts are always turned upwards!

It was in autumn 2004. On August 29th, Pierre had joined the Orthodox Metropolis of Romania in France. He began to celebrate again in communion with all the Orthodox churches. He needed a new church wardrobe, and we asked our hieromonk friend for an address. He told us about a monastery also dedicated to the Virgin. So we took to the road again to meet the Mother of God. No valley, no mountain, no forest. Just a mound mercilessly delivered to the sun, which however housed a new treasure of hospitality. We attended Vespers with the nuns. At the end, while we were worshiping the iconostasis, the gerondissa[84] was waiting for us with a smile that encircled her head. Thanks to the recommendation of our hieromonk, the next day Pierre found himself on a stool surrounded by three nuns, for measurements. This wardrobe earned us several back and forths. Each time we were welcomed as if at home. The Cypriot family had grown. Since then, we have often retraced the arid path from this arid place to this arid mound, which only their tenacity and their prayers have succeeded in transfiguring. They observe the same schedules as those in the nook of my mountain, which for the body is far from straightforward. The smile that encircles a head is the one with which I was able to take refuge after the ordeals of health or bereavement. *"Maria Mou!"*[85] she whispered, hugging me. This woman

---

[84] The higoumen of a nun's monastery.
[85] Term of endearment "My little Maria!"

also leads her community, with a perfect combination of rigour and love. We were introduced to the four corners of the monastery, the garden, new improvements there every year. We shared their services, their meals. What emotion when Pierre celebrated Vespers alone there in Greek. I couldn't help remembering his remark, during our first visit to Cyprus: "They are very nice, but you will never see a French priest celebrating in their churches!" It is obvious however, that none of this would have been possible without years of studying Greek. At the monastery no nun spoke English. We often laughed over coffee, Pierre always having a trick to amuse them. We also had fruitful exchanges on the life of the church, that of the saints. And several times a year we received a parcel from Cyprus with books that my dear, my very dear Gerondissa wanted to share with us!

24.

VISIT TO THE KATEKOUMENA[86]

I had made a friend who I had been meeting for a long time at the beach. The perfect Hellenic, high class! Perfect physique, perfect outfit, perfect family, perfect career. With innate ease and friendliness. Only his back that had seen operations was not perfect, and the sea was lifesaving for him too. Having learned that Pierre was a priest, he invited us in May 2005 to make a pilgrimage to the Katekoumena. First to his village church, dedicated to Saint Epiphanius of Cyprus, then on to the tomb of Saint Barnabas.

---

[86] Since 1974, 38% of Cyprus has been occupied by the Turkish, in the north of the island.

So here we are in a small overheated car without air conditioning, with our friend and his elderly mother who wanted to pray at her parents' grave. We were to meet former villagers who had come by bus to the spot. Serious border controls, then entry into this northern Turkish-occupied part of the island. At that time the first contrast was that of the dilapidated roads. Arriving at the village, we toured the places plunged into a form of abandonment. As if the occupants had decided to neglect both the infrastructure and the buildings. The granny was moved however, seeing this world where she had been at school and had spent a large part of her life. A few hundred metres from the church, we left the car, found the other pilgrims and walked together. On the way we saw a church transformed into a mosque. A little further on, we were allowed to enter what was left of the Church of Saint Epiphanius, that is to say, the ruins. Two armed Turkish soldiers then stood in front of the entrance. This sacred place had not been changed into another sacred place, but into a stable. Around us bales of straw, on the altar goat droppings. It was after clearing the manure that we sang the songs of the Resurrection, since we were in the post-Easter period. We must have been singing very badly, because the two soldiers asked us to leave. As I walked, I remember talking with a young girl who had known neither her grandmother's village nor the invasion. She told me that she wanted to live in peace with the young people of this part of the island. What the majority of the inhabitants did before the Turks invaded from the mainland. I found this dream all the more noble, as she and her friends were organising peace marches with young people from both sides. Back in our oven, we went to the village cemetery. I admit I received a violent shock. The mosque, the stable, the abandoned buildings, it was all part of the inevitable. But I never could have imagined that anyone would want to eradicate the roots of a culture by ravaging its cemeteries. Ransacked graves and broken headstones amid dry grass. In order to know that I was not dreaming, I took pictures. Of the grandmother painfully straightening the cross of the family tomb, so that we could sing the stanzas for her deceased who, to say the least, did not disturb anyone. Overthrown in our turn, we left for the chapel of Saint Barnabas. I literally watered the tomb of the Apostle of Cyprus with my tears. On the way back, I launched into this air of bravado: "I will not come back, until they give us back our territories!" This is what is called an accomplished integration! As for our barn, the former parishioners contributed and managed to completely renovate it. In 2019 our friend sent me the video of the first parish feast of Saint Epiphanius. Too bad for the goats, they will go elsewhere! And the granny? What happened to the mother? After living for a long time at home, singing her prayers alone, that year she entered the monastery where the hegumen is German. Regardless of anything, our Cypriot friends have a sense of universal orthodoxy!

25.

NEW FRIENDS

2004 was a turning point, because Pierre was laying the foundations of his Besançon parish, with all that entails as a commitment. His stays have become rare too, even shortened on several occasions. At that time, Easyjet operated daily Larnaca-Basel flights at very low prices. This allowed him to leave after 10 days, when he had planned for 15, as the parish needed him. The first time I had a hard time accepting it. By "chance", the next Sunday, at the home of my 'family below', the presbytera said that in Cyprus, when a priest was ordained, he took off his wedding ring. Which symbolised that the main marriage was now with the parish. However, the priests do not love their wives or their families any less. But they have been entrusted with the responsibility of a flock of which they are the guarantors before God. It helped me a lot. Especially since a few days later, my Cypriot confessor told me: "Don't forget that with your soul's balance sheet, you will be alone before Christ! Which, by the way, will reassure widows, bachelors or divorced! I realised that day that the conquest of our hypostasis was essential, whatever the external circumstances which could change at any time. With regard to hypostasis, I realised that this is a state beyond that of the individuation that the great psychiatrist C.G. Jung[87] speaks of. Because the individual, or rather the person, faces the most perfect Person the world has ever known: the God-Man. The key to respecting both the human and the divine, which is gymnastics, not to say a form of permanent cross. Sometimes it is also essential to be alone when you make a pilgrimage or attend a meeting, because the reactions and interactions

---

[87] Swiss doctor and psychiatrist, 1875-1961

are not the same. When in 2010 after my back operation, I returned to writing, I must even admit that this temporary loneliness suited me. Indeed, if I can correct a new book as a couple, I can only write it by being alone.

The organisation of my life revolved around the capacity of my body to travel, to take on the heat, the services, the pilgrimages to the nook of my mountain and of course, writing. So I had spartan schedules. To avoid the already overwhelming sun from 9:00 am, I got up at 4:30. I did my physiotherapy, my prayers, and after breakfast, I went to the beach to swim. I chatted a little, either with my Cypriot friends or with my fishermen. Back around 9:30 a.m. when the first tourists showed off their sunscreen. Shower, then some shopping. Every time I went downtown, I went to see Saint Lazarus. Each time with the same grateful emotion. After lunch, I would write, as my spine would allow. On Monday at 5:00 p.m., I had a reflexology session with a reflexologist who had a gift and was a great help to me during cancer treatments. The price for Maria was 20 euros, fixed for life! We quickly became accomplices. An increasing number of post reflexology sessions on the balcony at nightfall. With the dog who yelled tirelessly to demonstrate his disapproval of our philosophical debates. He wasn't yet 30 when I met him. Rather suspicious of the ecclesial world, he had a spiritual maturity filled with curiosity. Intuitive, funny, sincere, he was very attached to the Holy Scriptures. A bon vivant too, a nature lover. It's amazing what we were able to undo and remake in the world during these evenings. Over time I got to know the rest of his family, each one more eccentric than the other, and so endearing. I miss this "madhouse" as he liked to call it. We shared during all those years the worries and ordeals that both of us had gone through. Before an operation or during a stroke far from my island, he would go to my little Byzantine chapel, make a video and send it to me. But the most beautiful gift he gave me was Great Resurrection Saturday. Amongst us, this phenomenon is either ignored or mocked. On Easter night in Jerusalem in the Basilica, the Greek Orthodox Patriarch enters the tomb alone. He waits in prayer for Christ to light his candles. He then emerges with the famous

"Agios Phos"[88] which spreads at full speed over the faithful, in turn lighting the candles of the Resurrection. To date, as soon as the Agios Phos has arrived, the news is spread by Greek and Cypriot TV news. Planes from Orthodox countries immediately bring this light back to their respective countries. My reflexologist, who does not go to churches, however, leaves for the airport. One of his former air steward colleagues, as well as the staff who work there, are the first to light their candles. He then calls his relatives, announcing that he is bringing back this gift from God. The very one who made me happy to celebrate the Easter date with those whom on my first trip I described as uncivilized! Once again, The Holy Light did not make me better, but it was an experience of such Tenderness, that I thank my benevolent friend with all my heart.

Dinner was followed by a phone call with Pierre, then I listened to my precious Radio Kiti. After the broadcast of the Compline, I went to bed.

Often between two pages of writing, I would

---

[88] Holy Light

go chat with friends. I particularly liked going to the icon shop of a priest we had met in 2001. I sat down, he made me my tea, and off we went for hours of discussions. Once again imbued with the simplicity of people who know how to love. Over time I have shared some of the dramas of his life, including the cancer that took away one of his beloved daughters. I loved his kind smile, as well as the many uplifting little stories he told me with humour. I miss the shop too...

And then there was my crazy hairdresser whose turbulent fate I discovered over the years in his salon. Surrounded by his own paintings and fashion photos. He often made me a herbal tea and we took the time to be together. Because in Cyprus, it's still something we know how to do! Young, then married and father to three children, he had lived in England. He attended neither church nor monastery, but their home was next to the Monastery of St. John the Baptist at Maldon[89] in the blessed days of St. Sophrony. His children had often jumped the fence to play in the monastery garden. This is how my

---

[89] In Essex.

hairdresser met this contemporary saint. One of the particularities of the saints is that they are universal in their approach to each being, with a deep respect for their uniqueness. My hairdresser began to become attached to this walking fire that was Archimandrite Sophrony[90]. One day with his wife, they decided to leave to make their fortune in Australia. The Archimandrite was saddened by this news. He who seemed to read into the future, had advised him not to leave. It was with tears in his eyes that my friend recounted the farewell scene. The Archimandrite just hugged him. Moments of love so intense that made him secretly wish to remain with the man of God. In Australia his wife left him, and instead of making a fortune, he lost everything. So he returned with his son to Larnaca. One night his son was killed on a motorbike. My friend then began to wander, in the churches and monasteries of the region, bearded and dressed entirely in black. A few years later, he metamorphosed into this eternal lovesick teenager. He is once again unvarnished, sincere,

---

[90] Born in Moscow on 23.9.1896, and dying 11.7.1993 near Maldon. Canonised on November 29th 2019.

touching. Recently one of his daughters returned to the country and married a Frenchman lost in Cyprus. She gave birth to a son, so a grandson to my dear friend who finds a family again. I miss his salon too. I have never again found such an eccentric hairdresser. Who half the time cut my hair for free, believing that the value of our friendship exceeded that of his scissors! Yes, in Cyprus, I met several of these beings who, far from being rich, attached little value to money. "As long as I can pay for my bills and my meal!" he said to me, smiling with that childish smile, eternally peaceful, without being appeased.

26.

BUDDIES

Boys and girls! Like the one I met at the beach. Widowed, she came every morning with her two friends to soak her legs in the sea. The typical granny of the people, her voice resonant and well stamped. Tough despite the departure of her beloved man. One day she had her foot bandaged, and I asked her what had happened to her. Embarrassed by a bunion, she had tried to cut it out with a kitchen knife!

Another adorable granny, who was a swimmer, told me, in an equally audible voice, of the weekly theology courses given by the pope of her parish. Proud of her questions and the answers obtained.

There were also discussions with my grocer. He told me about his moving pilgrimages to Greece to Saint John the Russian[91] and Saint Ephrem the New[92]. Only in Cyprus do I talk about encounters with the saints while buying my toilet paper or my spaghetti!

The discussions with my pharmacist, also unforgettable. One might think that no one works on this island, and that everyone is talking! In fact, Cypriots have mastered the art of doing both, or even both at the same time! Also fervent about the Holy Mountain, his faith is expressed through his compassion for those who suffer. It was while flying to the rescue of one of these lost beings that he had a terrible car accident one Christmas night. From months of convalescence, for some time later, stung by a virus that had paralysed half of his face. The sight was distressing. Even more so for a pharmacist! Another one of those natures that ends up bouncing back, I just found him exactly as he was

---

[91] 1690-1730 young soldier of Peter the Great, Turkish prisoner.
[92] Martyred by the Turks close to Athens in 1426.

the first day! His wife, who adores the flowers with which the garden abounds, is exquisitely beautiful and gentle. Hard-working, peaceful, joyful people. Alive!

Another one of my beach buddies is less refined. As big as he was tall, he would arrive in the sea laughing, always laughing. After bathing, he'd give me tangerines when they were in season and tell me his principles for life "simple ones for simple happiness. Living alone, at peace, eating well, drinking well, smoking well and swimming well. Everything else is brainwashing!" I could add nothing to that and I never contradicted him.

And there was this East German, we met him on what was his first year on the road. A former sailor, he had come to spend his retirement in Larnaca. He dragged his slippers to the beach, delighted to exchange a few words in German. A brave fellow who liked to cool off with a good beer. He had a passion for birds. So that his proteges could fly freely, he had put bars on all the windows, including the balcony. His wife, not able to bear this caged life, often returned to Germany. When she left before I did, she came in tears asking me to watch over him. He ended up getting sick and dying in the hospital, luckily when she was present. Inkeeping with the dismal story, as there is no crematorium in Cyprus, his body was left to burn in Bulgaria. Returned in a green marble urn which was, according to his last wishes, emptied into the sea. A few days later the birds moved to one of our first neighbours. The one who used to walk his two dogs and his cat, and whose aviary had just been robbed. Alas a year later they had to find a new owner, because my boyfriend had a heart attack. He passed peacefully. Surrounded, as he would call them, by his family, that is to say his animals, in his small studio flat facing his aviary.

On the way to the sea, I ended up stopping at the houses that lined the path. First with a former municipal employee who gave me lemons from his garden. He shouted loudly too and always had advice to promulgate. His wife one Easter Sunday offered me a well-wrapped whole meal. I didn't know her very well, but in Cyprus, especially at Easter, we share meals!

A couple a little further along, with whom I became familiar. The lady who had breast cancer the same year I had mine. She passed away in 2013. I was the first to find out. Her husband had collapsed in tears on the terrace. Since then life has resumed and a young African takes care of his house. Often when I passed by, he showed me his garden and reserved fruit for me on the way back from the beach. He wasn't a rich guy either, but every day he left in his van to take meals to poor families.

In front of her house, an old loner called me regularly to accompany me to the sea. She was content to admire it leaning on her cane, repeating to me that life passed very quickly.

I also passed each morning in front of the home inhabited by the elderly or the disabled. I was joking with a woman who regularly asked me the same question: "What colour is your swimsuit Maria?" I answered black, but she always said it had to be blue!

In this home lived the one I secretly named: "my dear madman"! Lying in the generous air conditioning of the hotel opposite, he waited for the days to pass. He had a magnificent gaze. He told me about all the trips he thought he had made. He told me he was fine. Nourished, housed, bleached. He also spoke to me about his parish, his patron saint, because yes, in Cyprus even the mad have a patron saint! When I felt he was in need of them, I gave him money to buy cigarettes. Or I brought him fruit. One day I no longer saw him. I asked one of his less sympathetic helpers what had become of him. He answered me: "He went crazy, we put him in the mad house!" I dared to make my silly reply: "But wasn't he already mad?" Squealing smile: "Well, he's even crazier!" When it is his patron saint's feast, I do not fail to pray for my dear madman, so gentle, so elsewhere, so otherwise mad…

Sometimes coming back from the beach, I saw the Saint Raphael hearse in front of the home, and the passers-by, including myself, crossed themselves. Saint Raphael had come to pick up a boarder, for whom this last trip was most of the time a release. In Cyprus, death is not yet hidden, probably because we still believe in the resurrection!

27.

THE INCONNUS

Strangers whose names I don't know, passed on the roads. First this woman, one evening around 10 p.m. I had heard on my dear Radio Kiti that relics of Saint Spiridon[93] were being venerated in the church of Saint Jean Baptiste. I pulled out my map and spotted the neighbourhood. I swirled around Larnaca in vain, only to find myself in the middle of nowhere. It must be said in my defence, that I always rely on Pierre who is a walking map! After an hour of distraction, I stopped to review my journey, when a woman

---

[93] 270-348 Cypriot saint and thaumaturge.

passed in front of me. I stopped her and explained the purpose of my research. She then got into the car and guided me to the Saint Jean Baptiste church from which I was, needless to say, a thousand miles away! Not even a cat, which is rare in Larnaca. Church closed, which is even rarer, when there are relics. In general, the faithful take turns to keep watch. My unknown angel called a friend of hers, and we learned that the relics were in a village with the same name as the neighbourhood in question. I then accompanied my passenger. She had time to tell me that she was sad, because their house in the katekoumena had just been sold by the Turks to a German tourist. Another one who will never see the garden of her childhood again. I would add, however, that not all the gardens have been sold, or not yet. A friend who also wanted to see her old home again was received by the new owner who even gave her a bouquet of flowers picked from "her" garden.

It was not flowers that the stranger that I am going to describe collected, but cans of beer or soda. An old woman draped from head to toe in worn black clothes. These widows that we still meet in the countries of the South, and who seem to have always been old and widowed and dressed in black. The majority of them have the added bonus of the curse of being poor. Mine was pushing a big cart, rummaging through every bin for aluminum cans. I guess she sold them for a ridiculous sum. Her cart was always full, the ecological impulses having not yet reached the mind. Whatever the weather, she advanced with admirable courage. Sometimes I gave her a 20 euro note, which had to equal all the contents of her cart. But the old woman, with the gaze of beings who go through storms without moaning, neither jumped for joy nor told me about her miseries. She put the note in her apron pocket with dignity, murmuring: "God bless you, Lady!" One day I saw her no more and thought she had joined those I had already lost. Where we are supposed to suffer less. I even hoped that when I in turn knocked at the door of this kingdom, with my dirty heart, and the Big Boss asks me who I am, then a voice will rise: "It's Maria, and You blessed her already, next to my stinking garbage cans!"

The last guardian angel passed was on the road

to my dear mountain. The day before my trip, I had learned that our gerondas would leave the monastery early the next day. So I got up at dawn in order to arrive in time. In Limassol I fell into heavy traffic with queues at roundabouts. I had forgotten that traffic had become more difficult since the construction of a university. So I was chomping at the bit, literally and figuratively, in the line where I usually branched off. After half an hour of bumper to bumper, I decided to continue to the exit of the city. I would take the route we always took with Pierre on the way back. I knew the name of the village of Omodos, where we stopped to venerate a piece of the holy cross at the monastery. My traveling geography map failing me, I decided to rely on my almost obsolete sense of direction! Needless to say I missed the slip road and the more I drove on, the more this became obvious. Finally not recognising any landscape, I headed for the next exit only to engulf myself in a hamlet of recent constructions, far from the exorbitant prices of the city. I wandered in search of a good soul. Not even a cat, which I repeat is rare in Cyprus. Finally in a garden, I saw a man working and carrying bricks. I stopped to explain to him that I was going to my monastery and that I had got lost. My angel of the day dropped his bricks, his apron, his garden and got into his van telling me to follow him. After half an hour he signalled me the right exit by honking. I want to add that in accordance with recommendations, I always say the Jesus prayer while on the road. Especially on the one that leading to the heart of my love. Failing to make the traffic jams disappear, this attitude has – and I'm saying this for the atheists who I hope aren't annoyed yet – the advantage of helping me on the one hand to keep my calm, on the other hand not to give up!

28.

THE MURDERED GAZELLE

"Long slender legs, lioness hair and gazelle eyes. That's all I know of her." The man who described her like this is the latest to join my list of friends. A bon vivant with a booming voice. Once again, what I appreciate in him is his authenticity. There is no pretence about him. I have, since we were in the same building for a long time, got to know him better. As a young married man, he also travelled abroad, to Jersey more precisely. There he had opened a restaurant that did well, and he also set up his own driving school. After his divorce he raised his three children, and his family remained his main concern. No longer able to bear the year-round greyness, he returned to the land of light. Yet his island does not remind him only of bright memories. I quickly understood that there was a drama hiding behind this voice that I could recognise several streets before it arrived. One day he started giving me a few snippets. When I explained to him that I would write a book on Cyprus, he agreed to open up the box of terrible memories. He came one afternoon, half slumped on my couch, a glass of English beer in his hand. For five hours he spoke. He spoke very softly. No doubt to calm the pain revived by his story. His father ran a sweet shop in Nicosia. His family with its five children, three girls and two boys, lived in a village near Nicosia. At that time Greek Cypriot and Turkish Cypriot kids used to play together in the streets. Just like in the other villages where they sometimes invited each other to each other's weddings. But the situation remained unstable and looked likely to turn into a powder keg at any moment. As the rumours of war grew, the twelve-year-old gazelle was already proving an attentive sister to her little brothers.

In this month of December 1963, when the

intercommunity violence worsened, the father was in hospital for an operation. It was December 23rd. The mother was preparing for the Christmas party with her children, in their house in the village centre, surrounded by Greek Cypriot dwellings. They heard some big explosions coming from Nicosia but also from their village. The mother's brothers ran home to protect them all, armed with old hunting rifles. Other neighbours came too, to take refuge. Eventually there were about sixty of them in the big house.

When the Turkish Cypriots discovered the refuge, they started shooting. Georgia, the gazelle was on her knees tying her little brother's shoes. A shell hit her in the leg. One of those that, once in the flesh, explodes inside. Bloodied, the gazelle suffered hell. However, the ambulance could not transport her. The Turkish Cypriots fired on that vehicle, rescuing a dying 12-year-old child. So the mother, one of the uncles and a friend who was driving decided to cross the Turkish lines to take Georgia to the hospital. Their car was the target of new shots. The driver and the uncle barely managed to escape. The mother who remained with her daughter lay down on her to protect her. She was in turn riddled with bullets. Six hours in a bloodbath in the middle of the road, until Greek Cypriot soldiers from the nearby village managed to transport the two injured people to hospital. But Georgia with long slender legs, lioness hair and gazelle eyes succumbed to a generalised infection. It was Christmas Day.

Christmas 1963…

It is easy to imagine the distress of the family, in particular of the little brother who henceforth would have to tie his shoes without his beloved sister. As the mother was still hospitalised in a critical condition, it was decided to hide the fatal outcome of this tragedy from her. At this point in the story, the typical Cypriot party animal, a little rowdy, has mutated on my sofa into an eternally crushed little boy. Georgia's funeral was a nightmare. Her uncle Georgios, mad with remorse at not having been able to save her, broke the coffin with his cane to prevent her from being buried. The coffin opened with the gazelle's head rocking right and left. But the ordeal did not end there. The mother had to be spared and the horrible truth hidden from her. Also the visiting family exchanged their mourning clothes for colourful clothes at the hospital entrance. A crucifying masquerade for torn childish hearts. One day Makarios III came to the hospital to visit the victims of the conflict. He did not want the mother to be continually lied to. He offered his condolences for the tragic death of her daughter, "murdered for her homeland, Cyprus!" Perhaps it was better for this pious woman to learn of the tragedy from the mouth of this archbishop, so cherished by the people. However, the little boy on the sofa claims that it was not only the bullets that got embedded in his mother's body, that could not be removed, forever sealing the desolation in her heart. He remembers growing up with a dead sister, for whom the greatest share of love was reserved.

Yet life, as always, ended up taking back its rights! The noble and respected old lady Christalla, mother, grandmother and great-grandmother will celebrate her hundredth birthday, surrounded by her family on June 19 2022. As for the gazelle, no one doubts that she has joined the angels, where "there is no more pain or sighs, but eternal life"[94]...

---

[94] Orthodox funeral service

29.

"MARIA, WHAT EXACTLY ARE YOU LOOKING FOR?"

On this November morning, I went to the sea a little late. It was one of my last swims of the season. As soon as I arrived, I was challenged by a group of teachers, pillars of the beach all year round:

"Maria, how are things at home?"

"All good, why?"

"You don't know? In France it is war."

I thought it was a bad joke and laughed, only to find out there was really nothing funny. This date of November 13th, 2015 will remain engraved in the book of horrors. With a series of the deadliest attacks in France, perpetrated in the evening and claimed by the Islamic State. Terrorists had also perished, but the alleged mastermind was still on the run. A few days later just before my return, I heard on the news that he was surrounded in an apartment in Saint Denis in Paris. As he refused to surrender, his sentence was sealed, it was a matter of hours. I confess, for the first time in my life, to have wished for the death of a man!

That same evening I went to say goodbye to my little port. I sat down on my rock. Autumn was gently showing its sweetness. The tourists had left. The calm was reassuring. A few boats were still going out, others were coming back, after casting their nets. I love the hum of the engine of the fishing boats, it rocks me. Light waves brushed my feet. The sun was finishing its descent leaving a darkened sky, ready to welcome the princess of the night. Suddenly my little kingfisher, whom I call Barnabas, came to rest on the nearby rock. He tilted his jewel of a small head with its oversized beak, scanning the waves. Assessing the chance of bringing out another fish with one of his flashing dives. His turquoise-green feathers on his back, the red-brown ochre on his belly, reflected the perfection of the harmony of colours. He was so lively, so agile and so fragile at the same time that it brought tears to my eyes. I liked to think that he had come to say goodbye and wish me a good winter. I asked God to bless him in the immense puzzle of his sublime creatures. As soon as the sun hid behind the mountain of Stravrovouni, it flew away with small cries that I knew well. Flapping its thin wings above its foster mother.

Free!

I thought of the condemned man, surrounded on all sides. I wondered, as he went to present himself with bloody hands in front of the "Big Boss", if he would have an explanation for the monstrosity of his actions. Is it my little friend Barnabas, is it the splendour of this autumnal evening in this place so dear to my soul, but I found myself feeling sorry for him. Had he in his country had the chance to sit facing the soothing sea? Had he never heard the whispering of angels in the nook of a mountain? How could he take life in the name of the Giver?

I looked at the horizon. I compared it to my dark heart too, with its pile of filth. Her wish that a young assassin dies, in order to be reassured. It was then that I remembered this question, asked so many times since the freezing studio in the winter of 1999:

"Maria, what are you looking for?"

It was the queen-sea, the sea-queen, mother of life, who very gently, in rhythm, answered me without hesitation, sure of her message that she had been rolling in her foam since the depths of the centuries:

"God's mercy!"

Kyrie Eleison!

END

May 12th, 2022,
feast of Saint Epiphanius of Cyprus

POSTSCRIPT

DOXA TO THEO

November 2022

This postscript also starts at 11,000 metres above sea level, but this time in the "wrong direction", the one taking me away from my big pebble! My stay was shortened because Minus the Covid ended up catching me, and I had to postpone my departure. Barely able-bodied, I arrived with that kind of somatic and psychological fragility that always increases my emotions tenfold. So I rushed to my Saint Lazarus cathedral to thank him. Then, I turned to my best ally, the Cypriot sea, to eradicate the gunk from my bronchial tubes that Minus had attacked!

Sitting on a rock, I was approached by a young

man who gave me his backpack to go swimming. A Czech who was going to Limassol the next day to a conference about the soul and the body, before returning to Larnaca to lead his own workshop on the subject. A magnificent 40-year-old boy who looked 20 and who told me that he was finding a new balance and perspective thanks to the teachers he had met in this organisation. After six months of marriage his wife had left him, and he had lost his job. The ground beneath his feet was shaky when he discovered this group. Being one of the oldest, he in turn began to guide the lost. He touched me with his enthusiasm, his certainties, his drive to change the world. "A world that badly needed to be changed"; a conviction reinforced with each of his meditations as they gave him new energies. I told him that when I meditated, I always came up against my own bullshit. It was then that I realised that at his age, this was not the case at all! I also realised how much the encounters on "the island of all saints" had introduced me to this "metanoia". The Greek word for penance. By no means self-flagellation but, as my Cypriot confessor calls it: "A change in noùs". The word "noùs" when translated by the intellect, is relegated to only a Cartesian interpretation of the word. Instead, it refers to the deep heart, the core being, of which all orthodox asceticism is attempting to change the direction.

Blessed synchronicity, because the next day a little embodied example was going to reveal to me once again the liberating power of this approach.

I must go back to 2006, when the faithful and the clergy elected the new Archbishop of Cyprus. I, together with one of my priest friends, had favoured a candidate who was not elected. We had duly fallen into the worldly ways of criticism, even of mockery, concerning the winner, who over the years went on to reveal himself to be a great archbishop. Juggling between firmness and gentleness, an ability to coexist for a while with a communist government, a commitment to young people, consolidating the autocephalous Cypriot church by restoring all the bishoprics who'd been cut off by the Roman Catholics during the Frankish occupation. A special closeness with the faithful, that always showed itself in simplicity and humility. A witness during the pandemic, getting vaccinated publicly to show his gratitude to science. Supportive during the economic crises experienced by his dear homeland. But above all, a huge support for those most in need. The long illness that had been gnawing at him for years had just taken his toll that morning when I returned to my friend's house:

"You see, Maria, we criticised him, we made fun of him, and I apologise, because he was the best archbishop we had. He died penniless, because he gave everything to the poor! You know, Maria, why Christ says don't judge? Because you never know what's in a man's heart!" This "confession" shook me, as though I had entered his shop that morning so as to hear his words and I replied:

"Thank you Father, this truth sets me free. I too need to apologise for my gossip!" Tearful smiles, communion of sincere hearts. God it was good! God it was sweet! Because the acknowledgment of sin, the primary meaning of which is to miss the mark, is immediately followed by my famous "Kyrie Eleison!" Metanoia breaks down the locks to the heart and opens the door to God's mercy. Two central columns of Orthodox mysticism, as I discovered them in Cyprus. Gratitude, that other pillar, then invites itself in as a crowning glory. Doxa To Theo, Glory to God!

A few days later, the day before the feast of Saint John Chrysostom, I attended the funeral of our good Archbishop Chrysostom II by watching it on television. Once again, the power of the rite with its symbols, so many bridges that connect the visible world to the invisible world, literally pierced me. Patriarch Bartholomew, other patriarchs, metropolitans, bishops, priests, monks, nuns and other faithful were present. Among them, the President of the Republic of Cyprus; right next to Archbishop Chrysostom II in his open coffin, dressed in his liturgical vestments. In the midst of his people and before the altar, he concelebrated one last time on Earth, while already participating in the celestial liturgy. My very first reaction was again mundane:

"I hope the tourists are on the beach and not watching TV because they will find it macabre!"

Absolute and stunning antinomy:

The first of the church with his gleaming mitre stretched out like the last of mortals. But if the sting of death had lost none of its arrogance, the light of the rite in that brilliant church of Saint Barnabas in Nicosia already oozed the victory of the Resurrection. And if the pain remained very human and real, the appeasement of hope found its place in an equally palpable way. I once again touched, through this television screen, tool of our technology, the Heart of the intact Orthodox Tradition:

"By His death, He conquered death, to those who are in the tombs, He gave Life!" That resounding Easter Night troparion!

Patriarch Bartholomew, visibly moved, before opening the procession of those who would come to kiss the hand of Archbishop Chrysostom II one last time, said a few words. Above all, he recalled this other foundation, regardless of any human deviations from it, that:

"Christ was the only bishop of our souls!"

...

I have decided to close this postscript with a

more intimate anecdote about the young girl Georgia, to whose memory I dedicated this book:

Sitting on a terrace with her "little" brother, I gave him some copies of the book. He immediately began to read aloud the chapter devoted to his family and the tragedy that had bruised it. Stopping several times to cry with the authenticity of men who are not ashamed to be upset. Then he told me that his mother, the noble lady Christalla, also called the mother of Cyprus, had fallen asleep peacefully at the age of 100. Respecting her last wish, he arranged for her to be buried with the bones of his daughter Georgia. Upon opening the gazelle's tomb, he was surprised that Georgia's shoes were still intact after 60 years. The very second he told me this detail, I was "connected" to Saint Gerasimus of Kephalonia whose relics are incorruptible, and whose shoes are changed regularly. It is said that at night, he walks on his island continuing to bless and protect it. In the world, this is called a crazy old woman's fantasies, in the Orthodox Tradition, the communion of saints. A holiness that I am far from claiming as my own, since it's a communion that is open to all those who simply by their prayers – however unworthy they may be – click on the link that connects them to the Saints and... lesser saints! I imagined then that at night, the young girl "with the long, slender legs, the lioness hair and the gazelle eyes" was walking on my big pebble, continuing to watch over her little brother who not only knew how to cry, but had held onto his sunny child's laugh...

Doxa To Theo!

November 21, 2022, Feast of the Entry of the Mother of God into the Temple.

MARIA ANDREAS

Born in Algiers in 1950 (of Swiss-French nationality), Maria Andreas obtained her baccalaureate at *La Chaux-de-Fonds*. She spent two years travelling to Asia and North Africa in a campervan. After studying languages (Zürich, Cambridge), she worked for 25 years, as a French teacher, in a boarding school in German-speaking Switzerland. Forced to leave her students for health reasons, she moved to Bordeaux and resumed correspondence courses in orthodox theology and applied psychology. At that time, she was engaged in a long Jungian analysis with Professor Gérard Ostermann. During a year-long stay in Cyprus, she discovered the Greek language and the spirituality of Orthodox monasteries. It was then that she returned to writing, which had already won her, as a high school student, first prize in the 1967 Strasbourg European Essay competition.

www.mariaandreas.eu

Visit the website to see (and maybe even buy!) some wonderful gifts linked to this book. All designed by the author out of her love for the island and its people.

ALSO BY MARIA ANDREAS

Illness, My Complicit Enemy – Amazon, 2018
Arthritis, Osteoporosis, Breast cancer and Other Scourges – Amazon, 2019
Sparkles of Intensity – Amazon, 2020
The Tenth Plague – Huge Jam, 2021
Raphaela's 24-Hour Detox - Huge Jam, 2021
Cyprus, Your Heart, Your History – Huge Jam, 2022
Hook Up with Your Angel – Huge Jam, 2022

Be the first to know about new books
by signing up to the newsletter at

www.mariaandreas.eu.

Would you recommend this book? Please leave reviews on Amazon and Goodreads to help the author extend her readership...

www.ingramcontent.com/pod-product-compliance
Lightning Source LLC
Chambersburg PA
CBHW072052110526
44590CB00018B/3143